Human–AI Collaboration in Research

Human–AI Collaboration in Research: Practical Applications, Ethical Frameworks, and Future Directions positions human–AI collaboration (HAIC) as a defining feature of contemporary research ecosystems. The book examines the incorporation of AI across the research lifecycle, including research design, literature work, data collection and processing, analysis, interpretation, academic writing, and dissemination. It highlights the opportunities created by automation and generative systems, alongside the challenges raised for research integrity, accountability, transparency, privacy, and epistemic authority. Ethical and regulatory foundations are addressed through established frameworks such as the Belmont Report and the Declaration of Helsinki, as well as European governance instruments including the Ethics Guidelines for Trustworthy AI, the General Data Protection Regulation, and the EU Artificial Intelligence Act. By combining interdisciplinary perspectives from robotics, management research, and education, the volume translates abstract ethical principles into concrete research-relevant practices, offering a coherent and human-centred approach to trustworthy AI-supported inquiry.

The book offers original, research-ready frameworks and applied guidance for responsible HAIC, combining real-world case studies with practical strategies for trustworthy AI use. It equips researchers, educators, and management scholars with tools for human oversight, transparency, bias mitigation, and accountable AI-supported workflows, ensuring scientific rigour alongside innovation.

Human–AI Collaboration in Research

Practical Applications, Ethical Frameworks, and Future Directions

Ida Skubis
Daniel Xerri
Mladen Adamovic

CRC Press
Taylor & Francis Group
Boca Raton London New York

CRC Press is an imprint of the
Taylor & Francis Group, an informa business

First edition published 2026
by CRC Press
2385 NW Executive Center Drive, Suite 320, Boca Raton FL 33431

and by CRC Press
4 Park Square, Milton Park, Abingdon, Oxon, OX14 4RN

CRC Press is an imprint of Taylor & Francis Group, LLC

ISBN: 978-1-041-33163-6 (hbk)
ISBN: 978-1-041-33166-7 (pbk)
ISBN: 978-1-003-78640-5 (ebk)

DOI: 10.1201/9781003786405

Typeset in Times
by SPi Technologies India Pvt Ltd (Straive)

Contents

About the Authors

Ida Skubis is an Assistant Professor at the Silesian University of Technology in Poland. She holds a PhD in Linguistics and possesses Master's degrees in four languages. She has extensive professional experience in both academia and business, having held managerial positions in international companies. She currently serves as the CEO of the Housing Community. She is actively involved in interdisciplinary AI projects and frequently participates in international conferences. Additionally, she serves as a reviewer for international journals on AI-related topics. She has received numerous scholarships and awards for her scientific research, including a prestigious scholarship in France under the Marie Skłodowska-Curie Actions (Horizon Europe) for her research on the Ethics of AI.

Daniel Xerri is an Associate Professor in Applied Linguistics and TESOL at the University of Malta and the Chairperson of the ELT Council. He has published widely on different areas of English language education. He has co-edited more than ten books and authored over 250 publications. He has also delivered plenary talks and keynotes in 20 countries, and his research has been awarded international prizes. His main research interests are teacher research, educational technology, and professional learning. His most recent book is *The Rise of English as a Glocal Language: Reimagining its Role in an Era of Deglobalisation* (Springer, 2026).

Mladen Adamovic is a Reader in Global Management at King's College London. His recent research on AI in management focuses on algorithmic bias, ethnic discrimination in recruitment, and the implications of AI for equality, decision making, and leadership. He is an expert in business research methods and uses surveys, field experiments, and advanced quantitative analyses. His work has been published in more than 50 peer-reviewed journal articles, including *The Leadership Quarterly and Human Resource Management Journal*, and has also appeared in *Harvard Business Review*. As an award-winning scholar and highly regarded educator, he regularly delivers executive education.

Introduction

Foregrounding Human–AI Research Collaboration

INTRODUCTION

Artificial intelligence (AI) is no longer a peripheral research tool: it is increasingly embedded in how knowledge is produced, tested, and communicated across disciplines. It brings both promise and pressure. On the one hand, AI systems can extend researchers' analytical capacity, accelerate discovery, and support complex decision-making in environments that are difficult, dangerous, or information-rich. On the other hand, the growing autonomy and pervasiveness of AI amplify long-standing concerns about responsibility, bias, transparency, privacy, and human oversight – concerns that become even more acute when AI systems are used not only as objects of study, but as active contributors to the research process itself. In this sense, responsible research with and about AI is no longer optional; it is a condition for scientific legitimacy, public trust, and socially beneficial innovation.

It is recognised that AI is a major risk that could lead to detrimental outcomes, so research and development are needed to address it (World Economic Forum, 2024). While AI research is paramount, it is equally important to conduct research using AI in a responsible manner. This approach would enhance our understanding of the potential outcomes resulting from AI. Likewise, it will contribute to the transformation of research practices, more specifically by fostering methodological innovations and creating reliable AI tools for research

DOI: 10.1201/9781003786405-1

purposes. This demand positions AI and machine learning specialists, along with data analysts and scientists, among the top 10 fastest growing jobs for the period of 2023–2027 (World Economic Forum, 2024). Making progress in this area will require coordinated togetherness, interdisciplinary collaborations, and consistent actions (European Commission, 2025).

The appearance and continuous development of digital and intelligent technologies has not only revolutionised the way research is conducted but also redefined the epistemological foundations of knowledge creation. Research into AI ethics shows that a core set of five principles: transparency, justice (or fairness), non-maleficence, responsibility, and privacy, consistently appear in over half of published AI ethics guidelines (Hickok, 2021; Jobin et al., 2019). These principles capture the broad mandates of oversight, protection, and fairness in algorithmic systems, but without mechanisms of accountability and implementation, they risk remaining abstract (Hickok, 2021).

In the research context, the proliferation of generative AI models such as large language models means that these ethical precepts must be embedded throughout the research lifecycle, from question formulation, data collection and processing, to interpretation, authorship, and dissemination of results (Skubis et al., 2025). The expansion of digital platforms, cloud-based infrastructures, and algorithmic tools has lowered the barrier for data-intensive research, enabling novel forms of evidence and collaboration (Wołk et al., 2021). However, these same tools raise critical questions regarding authorship, intellectual ownership, and validity of AI-mediated findings, thus demanding new frameworks for academic integrity and governance in the digital era (Ortega-Bolaños et al., 2024).

Moreover, digital technology and AI are increasingly intertwined within research practices, giving rise to a more integrated and interdisciplinary model of knowledge production. Research on digital communication technologies identifies a typology based on synchronicity and interactivity, distinguishing four ideal types: broadcasting, corresponding, aggregating, and collaborating (Hazlehurst et al., 2023). These reshape how researchers collect, process, and communicate data. Such technologies enable innovative research tasks, including participant recruitment via social media, AI-assisted transcription, citizen science aggregation, and collaborative authorship across borders. The resulting intelligent research environments bring together automation, datafication, and human oversight within a single research ecosystem. Yet, as studies emphasise, technical efficiency must not overshadow ethical accountability or human creativity (Coeckelbergh, 2023; Floridi, 2019). Researchers must therefore critically consider how digital workflows influence power relations, data ownership, and the epistemic role of human judgement in co-producing scientific knowledge.

CHAPTER OVERVIEW

This book brings together a range of perspectives illustrating how digital and intelligent technologies are changing research ethics, integrity, and methodology across disciplines.

Chapter 1 analyses the role and ethics of humanoid robots in scientific inquiry, addressing interdisciplinary applications from archaeology to healthcare and reproductive science. It also analyses key ethical frameworks including the Belmont Report, the Declaration of Helsinki, and the European Union's (EU) *Ethics Guidelines for Trustworthy AI*, while assessing issues such as responsibility, transparency, bias, and informed consent under the EU AI Act. It also provides concrete examples of humanoid robots in research practice.

Chapter 2 investigates the integration of generative AI into teacher research and reflective practice. It introduces a conceptual framework that positions AI as a collaborative partner rather than a mere tool, supporting teachers through prompting reflection, assisting in data co-analysis, and sustaining iterative inquiry cycles. By exploring the synergy between human intuition and algorithmic processing, it demonstrates how AI can help educators uncover classroom patterns and refine pedagogical strategies. It argues that when grounded in a reflective partnership (Xerri, 2025c), generative AI empowers teachers to bridge the gap between theory and practice, fostering a more responsive and evidence-based approach to classroom-based research.

Chapter 3 provides a practical roadmap for management scholars seeking to employ generative AI systems, such as ChatGPT, within their research workflows. It systematically identifies specific research stages, from literature synthesis and hypothesis generation to data cleaning and drafting, where AI offers significant augmentative value. It critically assesses the benefits of enhanced efficiency against inherent limitations like hallucinations, data privacy risks, and algorithmic bias. By offering concrete recommendations for maintaining reliability and academic integrity, it provides management researchers with the necessary guidance to navigate the transition towards AI-supported inquiry while preserving human epistemic authority and rigorous scholarly standards.

The concluding chapter synthesises the shift from viewing AI as a tool to recognising it as a socio-technical research partner. It highlights how human–AI collaboration (HAIC) expands methodological possibilities while maintaining that human creativity and ethical judgement remain irreplaceable. It underscores trust calibration, transparency, and accountability as the pillars of effective symbiosis. It argues that HAIC represents a fundamental redesign of the research process, requiring metacognitive pedagogy and human-in-the-loop governance to ensure that technological augmentation consistently preserves human epistemic authority and research integrity.

CONCLUSION

This book argues for a human-centred and governance-aware understanding of AI in research that spans both embodied and generative systems, positioning HAIC as a fundamental redesign of the research process rather than a mere technological addition. Central to this argument is the conviction that ethics serves as an enabling condition for high-quality inquiry and scientific legitimacy rather than a barrier to innovation. Across the diverse cases presented – from humanoid robots navigating the complexities of deep-sea, nuclear, and reproductive contexts to generative systems acting as reflective partners for teacher-researchers – a core thematic architecture emerges. First, effective collaboration requires moving beyond simple task delegation towards a model of interdependent teamwork characterised by shared mental models and calibrated trust. Second, the integrity of the research enterprise must be anchored in meaningful human oversight, ensuring that accountability for AI-supported decisions remains clearly defined even as systems achieve higher levels of functional autonomy.

Consequently, this volume contributes to the global discourse on trustworthy AI by translating high-level abstract principles into specific, research-relevant practices. It offers a roadmap for operationalising collaboration: how to design robust oversight mechanisms, how to mitigate algorithmic bias and protect data privacy, and how to communicate AI's involvement with the transparency and traceability required for academic rigour. By exploring the tension between automation and human agency, the book addresses the urgent need for researchers to maintain epistemic authority – the human-in-the-loop – amidst increasingly automated environments. By bringing these cross-disciplinary perspectives into dialogue, this book equips researchers, educators, and practitioners with the conceptual tools and practical frameworks necessary to foster rigorous, ethically grounded, and human-centred collaborations that amplify rather than replace human creativity in contemporary research.

The Role and Ethics of Humanoid Robots in Contemporary Research Contexts

1

INTRODUCTION

Humanoid robots, which are designed to resemble the human body and interact in ways familiar to people, are becoming increasingly common in scientific work. These machines have developed from simple mechanical devices into complex systems capable of supporting researchers in both physical and cognitive tasks. As described by Tong et al. (2024), the development of humanoid robots brings together robotics, Artificial Intelligence (AI), neuroscience, biomechanics, and social sciences.

They are increasingly able to operate in varied environments using advanced motion planning, vision, and behavioural learning (Di Nuovo et al., 2013; Jafari et al., 2019; Jeffers et al., 2015; Wang et al., 2012). However, reaching higher levels of intelligence and general-purpose functionality continues to be a key technical challenge (Destephe et al., 2013; Skubis & Wodarski, 2023; Sugihara & Morisawa, 2020; Tazaki & Murooka, 2020).

These robots show promise across many sectors, including defence and military (Defense Science Board, 2016; Sadiku et al., 2024), disaster relief (Murphy, 2014, Murphy et al., 2021), space exploration (Diftler et al., 2011; NASA, 2023), manufacturing and logistics (Keith & La, 2024; Lackner et al.,

DOI: 10.1201/9781003786405-2

2024; Tubis & Rohman, 2023), assistance and caregiving (Lee et al., 2025; Sawik et al., 2023), healthcare (Cruz et al., 2024; Ragno et al., 2023; Sarker et al., 2021), marketing and advertising (De Mauro et al., 2022; Skubis & Damas, 2025; Skubis & Mosek, 2025), education (Deng et al., 2024; Newton & Newton, 2019; Wang et al., 2024), tourism and hospitality (Skubis, 2025a, 2025b), and entertainment (Jochum et al., 2017; Kober et al., 2012). They are also expected to play a larger part in everyday life and future industries (Darvish et al., 2023).

The development of humanoid robots has progressed through three major stages: from early bipedal walking (e.g., WABOT, WABIAN), through integrated sensing and control systems (e.g., Honda's ASIMO, Sony's QRIO), to the current times of dynamic, autonomous robots capable of complex behaviours (e.g., Boston Dynamics' ATLAS and Tesla's Optimus Prime) (Darvish et al., 2023; Tong et al., 2024).

According to the China Unicom Research Institute and the China Branch of BRICS Institute of Future Networks (2025), to advance humanoid robotics, three key areas need focus:

1. Hardware and Standards: improving durability, energy efficiency, and integration requires unified hardware standards and modular components. Supporting component manufacturers, especially in chips, sensors, and motors, is essential for reliability and scalability.
2. Perception and Technology: enhancing multi-modal perception (vision, touch, hearing) involves unified control frameworks, neuro-symbolic systems, and edge-cloud computing. A virtual-real training environment and open datasets can reduce development costs and improve learning.
3. Applications and Collaboration: deployment should start with simpler robots and tasks in sectors like automotive and pharmaceuticals, expanding as technology matures. International collaboration, standard-setting, and talent exchange are critical for sustainable, global progress.

The aim of this chapter is to analyse the role of humanoid robots in contemporary research through three illustrative case studies: OceanOneK, ARMstrong Dex, and emerging 'pregnancy robots', and to critically examine the associated ethical, legal, and governance challenges. Drawing on established research ethics frameworks and recent European AI regulation, this chapter aims to develop a human-centric perspective on how humanoid robots should be designed, deployed, and overseen in scientific and managerial contexts.

ETHICS OF AI HUMANOID ROBOTS IN RESEARCH

The ethical use of humanoid robots in research builds on established frameworks of research ethics. The Belmont Report (National Commission for the Protection of Human Subjects of Biomedical and Behavioral Research, 1979) and the Declaration of Helsinki (World Medical Association [WMA], 2013) stress principles of beneficence, respect for persons, and justice, which may also be relevant when humanoid robots are introduced into laboratory or field studies. These frameworks complement the *Ethics Guidelines for Trustworthy AI* (European Commission, 2019), which identify human agency, accountability, and transparency as critical conditions. Together, these guidelines underline that research with humanoid robots must preserve human responsibility for outcomes and prioritise participant protection over technological novelty.

One central concern is responsibility and accountability. When humanoid robots contribute to scientific discoveries or experimental work, questions emerge regarding authorship, intellectual credit, and liability in the case of errors or accidents. Calo (2015) argues that robotics challenges established legal doctrines because machines act with a degree of physical agency, yet liability must remain with identifiable human actors. Floridi and Cowls (2019) highlight accountability as a core ethical principle of AI, captured in their notion of explicability: technologies must not only be intelligible ('how does it work?') but also assignable in terms of responsibility ('who is responsible for the way it works?'). This framework underscores that without clear accountability, the other ethical principles guiding AI, such as beneficence, non-maleficence, autonomy, and justice, cannot be meaningfully upheld.

Another important aspect is human oversight and meaningful control. In the EU, the Artificial Intelligence Act (2024) (AI Act) requires demonstrable human supervision of high-risk AI systems, including research tools that could affect safety or fundamental rights. This principle is particularly relevant when humanoid robots operate in hazardous environments such as deep-sea archaeology or nuclear decommissioning, where failures could put human lives at risk.

Article 14 of the AI Act stipulates that high-risk AI systems must be designed and deployed so that natural persons can effectively oversee them during usage, to prevent or minimise risks to health, safety, or fundamental rights. It mandates oversight measures that are proportionate to the system's risk level, autonomy, and use context, including enabling people to understand the system's capacities and limitations, detect and address anomalies, avoid over-reliance (automation bias), correctly interpret outputs, and override or stop the system if needed.

From recent interdisciplinary research, scholars have attempted to clarify what effective human oversight of AI entails and under what conditions it can meaningfully work. For example, Sterz et al. (2024) identify four necessary conditions: a) causal power – humans must have real capacity to influence outcomes and intervene; b) epistemic access – sufficient understanding of what the AI is doing (including limitations, errors, anomalies); c) self-control – awareness of risks like automation bias and resisting undue trust; d) fitting intentions – moral responsibility and willingness to intervene when needed. This analysis also reviews how Article 14 of the AI Act aligns with these criteria but notes that many practical challenges remain for implementation.

Safety and risk management have been central to robotics ethics debates. ISO 13482 (ISO, 2014) defines safety requirements for personal care robots, while ISO/TS 15066 (ISO/TS, 2016) offers collaborative operation standards that can be applied to robotic (including) humanoid research platforms. ISO/IEC 23894 (ISO/IEC, 2023) extends this to AI risk management across the system lifecycle. Documenting hazards and protective measures according to such standards ensures that robots like OceanOneK, ARMstrong Dex or 'pregnancy robots', deployed in high-risk contexts, minimise the chance of harm while preserving experimental value.

Humanoid robots often capture sensitive information through multimodal sensing, raising privacy and data governance concerns. The General Data Protection Regulation (European Parliament & Council of the European Union, 2016) imposes strict rules on data minimisation, lawful processing, and informed consent, which apply whenever robots record human participants or bystanders. Mittelstadt et al. (2016) argue that transparency and consent are critical in algorithmic systems, reinforcing the point that researchers must disclose data collection practices and restrict secondary use. In clinical or quasi-clinical contexts, these requirements align with the Declaration of Helsinki's (WMA, 2013) provisions on research participant rights.

Recent studies on AI-driven leadership also highlight how humanoid robots influence management ethics and organisational decision-making. Research shows that while such systems are valued for efficiency and impartiality, they are viewed critically for lacking empathy, creativity, and moral reasoning – qualities essential for ethical leadership (Skubis, 2025a). These findings indicate that human oversight and emotional understanding remain indispensable in technologically advanced workplaces.

In particular, the case studies of Mika, the AI-driven CEO of Dictador (a luxury rum company in Poland), and Tang Yu, the virtual CEO of NetDragon Websoft (a Chinese gaming company), demonstrate practical implementations of humanoid or virtual humanoid leadership. Mika's role involves strategic data-driven decision support and brand representation, while Tang Yu oversees aspects of performance evaluation and operational efficiency, relying on real-time analytics to guide corporate actions. These cases show how AI can improve efficiency and data-driven decision-making, especially in tasks like process optimisation, market forecasting, and algorithmic analysis, while also raising concerns about the lack of emotional intelligence, limits of accountability in automated leadership, and the risk of over-reliance on algorithmic governance. Analyses within project management frameworks suggest that the most effective approach is a hybrid model, where AI supports analytical and operational tasks, and humans retain ethical judgement, empathy, and final responsibility (Skubis, 2025c).

A further ethical issue involves bias and fairness in robot perception systems. Buolamwini and Gebru (2018) showed that commercial facial analysis systems exhibit large disparities in error rates across skin tones and genders, a risk that could undermine data validity in research with diverse populations.

The anthropomorphic design of humanoid robots also creates challenges of over-trust and emotional attachment. Sharkey and Sharkey (2010) note that a human-like form can elicit misplaced confidence, particularly in vulnerable groups such as children or the elderly. Lewis et al. (2018) highlight the role of calibrated trust in human–robot interaction, stressing the importance of clear communication about system capabilities and limits. Trust repair mechanisms are necessary when robots fail, ensuring that participants do not develop unrealistic expectations.

Duffy (2003) and Złotowski et al. (2017) argue that human-like features foster emotional attachment and social attribution, which may distort participants' responses in research settings. For example, people may overestimate a humanoid robot's competence or moral agency simply because it looks or behaves like a human. This raises concerns about informed consent and the validity of research outcomes, as research participants may conflate the robot's programmed behaviours with genuine social interaction. Ethical research therefore requires that anthropomorphic elements be critically assessed for their influence on experimental integrity and research participant autonomy.

Beyond laboratory concerns, dual-use risks complicate ethical assessments. Sharkey (2012) warns that robotic systems designed for peaceful purposes can be adapted for autonomous warfare. Human Rights Watch (2012) similarly cautions against lethal autonomous weapons, arguing that such technologies undermine humanitarian law. Cummings (2017) observes that AI in defence contexts often develops faster than governance frameworks can adapt, raising the risk of premature or unsafe deployment. These debates are relevant to research robots like ARMstrong Dex, which, while designed for disaster response, could be militarised.

Labour and institutional readiness also raise ethical questions. Acemoglu and Restrepo (2020) found that industrial adoption of robots can reduce employment and compensation in affected sectors. While research robots do not directly displace workers, translational projects moving from laboratories to applied settings could contribute to similar trends. ISO/TS 15066 (ISO/TS, 2016) emphasises training and safe collaboration, reminding institutions that introducing humanoid robots requires new safety procedures, worker consultation, and skill development for students and staff.

Sex robots and intimate humanoids raise a distinct cluster of ethical issues that spill over into research design and public communication. Beyond safety and privacy, key risks involve the normalisation of instrumentalised intimacy, reinforcement of harmful stereotypes, consent confusion in human–machine encounters, and market-driven pressures that commodify bodies and relationships. Governance challenges include setting boundaries for content, marketing, and usage contexts; aligning innovation incentives with dignity and non-exploitation; and calibrating informed-consent language for trials involving intimate interactions (Devlin, 2018; Richardson, 2016; Skubis, 2024a, 2024b). Discourse studies further show that prompts, framing, and platform affordances substantially influence public judgements of sex-robot acceptability and risk, highlighting the necessity for careful terminology, transparency, and bias-aware communication in both lab studies and outreach (Sharkey & Sharkey, 2021; Skubis et al., 2023, 2025).

Using the Technology Acceptance Model, a survey of 14 top executives revealed cautious optimism: while robots can reduce labour shortages, operate continuously, and provide novel guest experiences, challenges remain around high costs, technological limitations, and the risk of losing the human touch. Ethical concerns focus on balancing efficiency with human-centred service, managing staff resistance, addressing biases in AI, and ensuring accountability when robots shape customer interactions and business practices (Skubis, 2025a). Complementing these findings, studies across tourism and hospitality document managerial and societal tensions around humanoid deployment, including role reconfiguration, guest experience, and fairness – key for study design and oversight (Skubis 2025b). At the policy level, analyses of EU roboethics guidance clarify how dignity, autonomy, and human oversight should constrain experimental use of humanoids, providing a regulatory compass for research protocols (Skubis, 2024c).

HUMANOID ROBOTS IN RESEARCH

OceanOneK (O2K) for Deep-sea Exploration

OceanOneK (O2K) represents a major advancement in underwater humanoid robotics, developed for deep-sea exploration with sophisticated features such as bimanual manipulation, stereo vision, and haptic human–robot interaction. Designed by a multidisciplinary team led by Oussama Khatib, the robot can operate at depths of up to 1,000 metres, significantly expanding the reach of underwater exploration compared to its predecessor, OceanOne. Unlike traditional remotely operated vehicles (ROVs), OceanOneK is designed for intuitive human–robot interaction. It features compliant, series-elastic arms with force sensors, stereo vision, and a human-like form that enhances operator control through telepresence. The robot's architecture allows users to 'feel' underwater objects in real time, enabling delicate manipulation of fragile artefacts or coral *in situ* – tasks that traditional ROVs often perform clumsily or destructively (Ackerman, 2016).

The robot enables precise and responsive manipulation of tools and objects underwater through haptic feedback, allowing researchers to interact with complex environments in real time. Following initial testing at Stanford University's AOERC Avery Pool, where its navigation, manipulation, and control algorithms were validated, OceanOneK embarked on multiple Mediterranean missions in 2022. These included dives to several notable sites such as the wreck of a P-38 aircraft (40 m), a Beechcraft Baron (67 m), the submarine *Le Protée* (124 m), a Roman shipwreck in Aléria (334 m), and the *Francesco Crispi* passenger ship (507 m). Its final mission off the coast of Cannes reached a record-breaking depth of 852 metres, marking the first instance of a humanoid robot physically touching the seafloor at such depth (Standford Robotics Lab, n.d.).

OceanOne's initial mission in 2016 to the wreck of *La Lune*, a 17th-century French flagship, demonstrated its capabilities in underwater archaeology. The robot successfully retrieved a fragile vase from the site under direct haptic control, demonstrating its dexterity and human–robot synergy. The success of such missions underlines the potential of humanoid underwater robots to enable unprecedented *in situ* research on coral reef ecology, marine archaeology, and underwater engineering – combining human cognitive abilities with robotic endurance and precision to lead interdisciplinary scientific research.

ARMstrong Dex for Disaster Relief and Hazardous Environments

ARMstrong Dex is a state-of-the-art humanoid robot developed by South Korea's Korea Atomic Energy Research Institute (KAERI) to operate in high-risk and hard-to-access environments such as disaster zones and nuclear facilities. Featuring a dual-arm hydraulic system, caterpillar tracks for mobility, and human-scale proportions, ARMstrong Dex is designed to perform a wide range of tasks that blend brute strength, fine motor control, and real-time decision-making – pushing the boundaries of robotic assistance in crisis response.

In a recent demonstration, the robot accurately threw a 500-ml water bottle into a barrel from 10 feet away, showcasing its trajectory planning, force modulation, and sensor precision. While seemingly simple, this test reflects a critical capability in disaster scenarios: delivering essential supplies like water, radios, or medical kits across obstructed or unsafe terrain – potentially saving lives when human access is not feasible.

ARMstrong Dex's manipulative strength was previously demonstrated through pull-ups with a 20 kg load and single-arm curls lifting around 40 kg, validating its hydraulic control system under resistance. These mechanical strength tests, coupled with refined feedback and control mechanisms, allow the robot to adapt dynamically between heavy-duty and delicate tasks from lifting rubble to precisely operating valves or connecting wires (Zilber, 2025).

The robot's human-compatible design enables it to navigate and function within existing infrastructure, corridors, control panels, and valve stations, while its caterpillar treads ensure stable movement over rough, debris-filled terrain. Controlled remotely, ARMstrong Dex keeps human operators at a safe distance, particularly valuable in nuclear decommissioning, one of KAERI's strategic deployment goals. The robot's capabilities are being transferred to companies like Victex for real-world application in dismantling nuclear power plants.

ARMstrong Dex is part of KAERI's broader robotics initiative, which also includes systems like TRAM, designed for indoor radiation monitoring, and RAM (engineered for semi-autonomous outdoor surveillance), aiming to enhance human safety, operational efficiency, and precision in high-stakes industrial settings. Its development demonstrates how robotics can support humanitarian missions and hazardous technical operations (Williams, 2025).

Despite some public debate about the militarisation of rescue technology, ARMstrong Dex's primary vision remains clear: to augment human response capabilities, deliver life-saving tools when and where they are needed most, and minimise risk to first responders. Its evolution signals a future where agility, dexterity, and strength converge in humanoid machines to tackle the world's most dangerous challenges (Williams, 2025).

Pregnancy Robots: Artificial Wombs in Humanoid Form

Another controversial development in humanoid robotics is the so-called 'pregnancy robot', a life-sized humanoid designed to replicate the gestational process. Announced by Dr. Zhang Qifeng, founder of Kaiwa Technology in

Guangzhou and affiliated with Nanyang Technological University, the project envisions robots equipped with an artificial womb embedded in their abdomen. Although these robots are described as using artificial amniotic fluid and hose-based nutrient delivery to sustain a foetus for up to 10 months and enable live birth (Buontempo, 2025; Malayil, 2025), the credibility of this technology has been questioned (Lanese, 2025).

Unlike conventional neonatal incubators, which only support partial gestation, the pregnancy robot aims to replicate the entire process from conception to delivery. At the 2025 World Robot Conference in Beijing, Qifeng emphasised that laboratory work has already shown artificial wombs to be scientifically feasible, citing prior experiments such as the successful support of a premature lamb in an artificial 'biobag' in 2017 (Malayil, 2025). The humanoid form is intended to allow real human–robot interaction during pregnancy, providing a more lifelike surrogate experience.

With an anticipated cost of under 100,000 yuan (approximately $14,000), the robot is marketed as a more affordable alternative to human surrogacy, which in countries like the United States can reach $100,000–200,000. The commercial aim is clear: to make parenthood accessible to couples struggling with infertility or to those seeking alternatives to traditional gestation.

Beyond reproductive applications, pregnancy robots could also serve as research platforms. They may offer scientists unprecedented opportunities to study embryonic development in controlled, artificial environments, potentially accelerating breakthroughs in reproductive medicine, developmental biology, and bioethics. Such a system could even allow comparative research between natural and artificial gestation or provide data on the impacts of different nutrient regimes and environmental factors on foetal development.

However, the ethical and legal challenges are profound. Fundamental questions remain unanswered: How will fertilisation and implantation occur? Who holds parental rights and responsibilities when a robot carries a human child? What safeguards will prevent misuse, such as commodification of human reproduction or exploitation of vulnerable populations? Critics also highlight risks of dehumanisation, where children born via artificial wombs might be regarded differently, and concerns about the commercialisation of life itself. Moreover, the anthropomorphic design could create false emotional attachments, raising dilemmas about autonomy, consent, and the social status of humanoid surrogates.

While Kaiwa Technology has initiated discussions with provincial authorities in China to explore policy frameworks, the international community remains divided. Some see the pregnancy robot as a game-changer for infertility treatments, while others warn that it represents one of the most ethically fraught applications of humanoid robotics where the line between biological reproduction and technological intervention risks becoming blurred.

CONCLUSION

Humanoid robots now play an increasingly important role in both scientific and managerial research, supporting humans in complex, often high-risk environments. The examples of OceanOneK, ARMstrong Dex, and 'pregnancy robots' show how advanced design and human–robot cooperation can expand the possibilities of exploration, healthcare, and reproductive science. At the same time, these developments raise important questions about responsibility, transparency, and human oversight.

This chapter shows that ethical governance must go beyond technical compliance. Following the AI Act (2024), ISO safety standards, and long-standing principles such as those in the Belmont Report and the Declaration of Helsinki, it argues that humanoid robotics must remain firmly human-centred. Responsible use of these technologies depends on clear accountability, respect for human dignity, and the protection of participants and society.

As humanoid robots become part in research infrastructures, workplaces, and even intimate or reproductive contexts, ethical frameworks must adapt to address new forms of risk, agency attribution, and human–machine dependency. Robust oversight mechanisms, interdisciplinary collaboration, and continuous monitoring of societal impact will be essential to prevent misuse, unintended harms, and erosion of fundamental rights.

Moreover, this chapter highlights that ethical challenges are not uniform across all applications: underwater archaeology, nuclear decommissioning, managerial decision-making, and artificial gestation each introduce distinct governance demands. Future research must therefore adopt domain-specific ethical guidelines while maintaining universal principles of justice, beneficence, and human autonomy. This includes developing clearer regulatory pathways for emerging technologies, enhancing transparency of algorithmic processes, and strengthening public engagement to ensure societal legitimacy.

The future of humanoid robots in research and management will depend not only on technological progress but on the capacity of institutions, policymakers, and developers to incorporate ethical reasoning into every stage of design, deployment, and evaluation. Maintaining this alignment between innovation, ethics, and public trust will determine whether humanoid robots become empowering tools for human flourishing or sources of new inequality, risk, and ethical uncertainty. The future of humanoid robots in research and management will depend on maintaining the balance between innovation, ethics, and public trust.

2 Facilitating Teacher-researchers' Reflection on Classroom Inquiry Through Generative Artificial Intelligence

INTRODUCTION

Reflective practice has long been recognised as a cornerstone of teacher learning and professional growth (Farrell, 2016). Within language education in particular, it serves as the critical bridge between classroom experience and pedagogical development, enabling teachers to interrogate their assumptions, evaluate evidence from their teaching, and adapt their practices in response to complex learner needs. Yet reflection is not simply an individual cognitive act. It thrives when dialogic, scaffolded, and situated within supportive communities of practice. In this sense, teacher research provides a natural home for reflection: it positions educators as inquirers into their own classrooms, embedding reflection into a systematic examination of teaching and learning (Xerri, 2017, 2019, 2021, 2022; Xerri & Pioquinto, 2018).

At the same time, teacher-researchers frequently struggle to sustain systematic reflection alongside the everyday demands of teaching (Cochran-Smith & Lytle, 2009; Zeichner & Liston, 2014). Their reflective accounts often risk

DOI: 10.1201/9781003786405-3

remaining descriptive rather than critical, unless supported by intentional scaffolds such as guided prompts, collaborative dialogue, or structured feedback (Senese, 2017). Moreover, the rise of digital technologies has reshaped both the possibilities and pressures of reflective practice. While self-regulated digital reflections often remain superficial, structured and dialogic, forms of engagement tend to yield deeper insights and stronger professional learning outcomes (Fessl et al., 2023).

It is in this context that generative AI emerges as a potentially transformative partner. Such tools offer teacher-researchers on-demand reflective prompts (Turakhia et al., 2024), support for synthesising complex data sets, and fresh perspectives that might not be immediately apparent through human observation alone (Abunaseer, 2023; Hutson, 2025). Research indicates that AI-driven reflective scaffolds can help teachers move from surface-level recall towards multilayered critical reflection, particularly when combined with collaborative dialogue and human judgement (Arefian et al., 2024). By acting as a valuable reflective partner for teacher-researchers, generative AI facilitates a more structured and in-depth reflective practice that contributes to professional growth and improved educational outcomes (Xerri, 2025c).

This chapter situates generative AI within the long-standing tradition of reflective teacher research. It begins by outlining the theoretical foundations of reflective practice and its critical role in classroom inquiry, before introducing the affordances of generative AI for teacher reflection, showing how the technology can act not as a replacement for teacher judgement but as a reflective partner that scaffolds noticing, co-analysis, and iterative cycles of inquiry. Culminating in the Reflective Partnership Framework (RPF), this chapter explores how generative AI can enrich teacher research in language education by enhancing the reflective process forming part of classroom inquiry. This chapter argues that harnessing generative AI critically and responsibly can amplify teachers' reflective capacities, strengthen the research–practice nexus, and support the ongoing transformation of teacher identity in a rapidly changing educational landscape.

THE SIGNIFICANCE OF REFLECTIVE PRACTICE FOR TEACHER LEARNING

Reflective practice is widely regarded as a cornerstone of teacher learning, but its significance lies in how it shapes awareness and professional growth. A synthesis of 116 Teaching English to Speakers of Other Languages studies shows that teachers benefit most when reflection is dialogic, emerging through discussion groups, post-observation conferences, and collaborative inquiry rather than being confined to individual written accounts (Farrell, 2016). Similarly, Lukáčová (2020) notes that while pre-service teachers often acknowledge reflection's importance, they struggle to move beyond descriptive accounts of teaching. She stresses the need for feedback sessions, guided questioning, and digital tools such as e-portfolios to help deepen analysis. Together, these studies suggest that reflective practice is not a solitary act but a structured, socially mediated process that allows teachers to interrogate their experiences and develop a more nuanced understanding of their pedagogy.

A second dimension of reflective practice relates to the ways it can be modelled, scaffolded, and facilitated. Triangulating different reflective approaches – such as dialogues, belief maps, and video-stimulated recall – brings to the surface both tacit and explicit teacher beliefs, strengthening confidence and pedagogical awareness (Johannessen, 2024). Portfolios, too, have been shown to be valuable when appropriately supported. As Scoupe et al. (2024) argue, portfolios help pre-service teachers link classroom experiences with employability competences like expertise, lifelong learning, and social skills, though their value depends on structured guidance and mentoring. What emerges is that reflective practice becomes transformative not simply by being encouraged but by being supported with intentional scaffolds that make implicit beliefs and skills more visible, actionable, and connected to broader professional demands.

The role of context and environment is equally critical. Reflection thrives when it is relational and situated within safe, supportive settings that promote trust and open dialogue (Marshall et al., 2022). Skilled facilitators who model reflective qualities and encourage collaborative meaning-making can help practitioners move beyond private rumination towards collective learning. Marshall et al.'s (2021) literature synthesis highlights the triggers that often spark reflection – such as uncertainty or puzzling experiences – and the importance of autonomy and confidentiality in sustaining it. These studies collectively illustrate that reflection is not merely an internal cognitive act; it is deeply influenced by the conditions in which it takes place and the dispositions of practitioners. Without supportive environments and appropriate triggers, reflection risks remaining superficial rather than critical and transformative.

Underlying reflective practice are key attitudes and dispositions that give it substance. Farrell (2023) insists that reflection is not reducible to a set of strategies but depends on cultivating Dewey's (1933) attitudes of open-mindedness, responsibility, and wholeheartedness. This view resonates with Chetcuti (2002), who links reflective growth to Dewey's (1933) classic triad of dispositions alongside Schön's (1983) concepts of reflection-in-action and reflection-on-action. These qualities allow teachers to interrogate assumptions, evaluate consequences, and commit to professional inquiry, gradually shaping their personal teaching philosophy. Similarly, Russell and Martin (2017) challenge the dominance of technical rationality in teacher education, calling instead for an epistemology of practice that privileges mindfulness and Munby and Russell's (1994) notion of the authority of experience. Such perspectives make clear that reflective practice is not simply a tool for professional development but a way of being that positions teachers as active, critically aware learners within their own classrooms.

Reflection is increasingly seen as an evolving and ethically charged process. Russell and Martin (2019) advance the idea of an ethical reflective turn in self-study research, arguing that teacher educators must frame reflective practice not only around pedagogy and content but also around ethics, where caring, trust, and integrity are central. Cornish (2024) echoes the idea of progression, describing how teachers often move from technical reflection focused on classroom management to critical reflection that centres on student learning, aided by scaffolds such as professional standards and Brookfield's (2017) four lenses: students' eyes, peer perceptions, theoretical perspectives, and personal experience. Yet Oates and Mynott (2025) caution that dominant human-centred models risk making reflection superficial and performative. They propose instead a more-than-human framework that acknowledges the material, technological, and organisational dimensions of practice. Thus, reflection is not seen as a fixed practice but as one that continually evolves, requiring teachers to expand its scope, attend to ethical imperatives, and adapt to broader contexts of change. While it plays a central role in teacher learning, if reflection is to move beyond an individual habit it must be embedded in systematic forms of inquiry that link teachers' professional growth to research. This makes it necessary to explore the intersection of reflective practice and teacher research.

REFLECTIVE PRACTICE AND TEACHER RESEARCH

Teacher research has long been recognised as a vehicle for embedding reflection into professional learning, though scholars stress that it requires systematic design and sustained support. For example, reflection within teacher research cycles enables pre-service teachers to move from focusing narrowly on their own performance to examining student learning outcomes, thereby building confidence and professional agency (Smith et al., 2010). Dana and Yendol-Hoppey (2010) similarly argue that inquiry-oriented learning communities, structured with clear protocols, make reflection more systematic and collaborative by providing space to challenge assumptions and sustain inquiry. However, reflective practice in teacher education often remains at the level of recall rather than deep analysis, underscoring the importance of repeated opportunities such as action research and peer questioning to cultivate transformative habits (Senese, 2017). In fact, Jones (2024) stresses that reflection must be systematically embedded in professional practice, supported by mentors who scaffold learners' zones of proximal reflection; using action research and other approaches, novices can progress from surface-level repetition to deeper, critical, and transformative reflection that bridges theory and practice. These perspectives converge on the point that teacher research is not merely about producing knowledge, but about embedding reflective practice in ways that reshape both pedagogy and identity.

A growing body of literature demonstrates how action research in particular has become central to developing reflective capacities among teachers (Xerri, 2025d). Action research positions teachers as both practitioners and investigators, empowering them to identify and solve problems in their own classrooms (Osmanović Zajić & Maksimović, 2020). Findings indicate that reflective competence tends to increase with teaching experience, as seasoned educators show stronger skills and attitudes towards inquiry (Osmanović Zajić & Maksimović, 2020). Parkison (2009) echoes this view in the context of pre-service education, where field-based action research assignments encouraged novices to question assumptions and evolve into democratic educators. Hagevik et al. (2012) further show that action research helps pre-service teachers move from routine reflection towards dialogic forms, although transformational levels are reached only with time and collaborative structures. These studies affirm that action research provides not only methodological tools but also a developmental pathway for teachers' reflective growth.

Action research has emerged as a particularly powerful framework for linking reflective practice with professional growth because it bridges the often-cited gap between theory and practice. It allows teachers to step back from entrenched traditions, critically interrogate their habits, and generate new professional knowledge through collaborative, inquiry-driven processes rooted in both theoretical perspectives and classroom realities (Apelgren et al., 2015). This bridging role is especially evident in teacher education, where Cabaroglu (2015) demonstrates that pre-service teachers can reconceptualise classroom challenges as opportunities for systematic inquiry. By engaging in iterative cycles of planning, acting, observing, and evaluating, student teachers not only enhance their self-awareness and problem-solving abilities but also gain confidence as they progress from routine or technical reflection to more dialogic and transformative forms. Maxwell (2024) reinforces this view by showing that when action research is supported with structured feedback, it pushes practitioners beyond surface-level technical observations towards deeper critical reflection and transformative learning. Action research is, therefore, not merely a research approach but a dynamic pedagogical process that embeds inquiry within practice, enabling teachers to evolve as reflective professionals.

Beyond individual inquiry, collaborative frameworks have been shown to amplify reflection by creating supportive professional communities. For example, online collaborative action research has been shown to enable English as a Foreign Language (EFL) teachers to deepen reflectivity, build trust, and link theory to practice (Fathian & Farahian, 2021). Similar findings are reported by Qing-li et al. (2019), who demonstrate how collaboration between pre-service teachers, tutors, and teacher educators fosters critical reflection despite challenges such as limited time and uneven modelling. The potential of reflective collaboration also extends to design-based research (DBR). Reflective dialogues within DBR partnerships promote shared goal-setting and co-design, although they are often complicated by theoretical and institutional constraints (Schäfer, 2025). Meanwhile, Dunn et al. (2023) argue that teacher leadership is a crucial factor in bridging research and practice, with teachers serving as reflective leaders who mediate knowledge within communities of practice. When reflection is socially mediated, it not only deepens individual inquiry but also strengthens the research–practice nexus.

Teacher research also creates spaces for teachers and learners to co-construct knowledge. Hanks (2021) insists that practitioner research should be fully inclusive, engaging learners as co-researchers who puzzle and theorise alongside teachers through multimodal methods such as poster creation. This resonates with Miller et al.'s (2021) interpretation of exploratory practice, which frames both teachers and students as practitioners of learning who investigate classroom puzzles collaboratively. Soomro's (2018) case study supports this perspective, demonstrating that exploratory practice embeds inquiry into everyday teaching in ways that are feasible, collaborative, and growth-oriented. At the same time, entrenched transmission-based approaches persist among pre-service teachers, suggesting that reflective collaborative action research is needed to disrupt routine habits, though change can be hindered by discipline pressures and low self-efficacy (Al-Qura'n, 2004). This implies that reflective practice within teacher research is most powerful when it is co-constructed, inclusive, and oriented towards transforming classroom realities.

Various methodologies within teacher research further illustrate the versatility of reflection. Autoethnography, for example, is shown to help international teachers navigate shifting professional identities across sociocultural contexts (Sahling & De Carvalho, 2021). Journals likewise play a crucial role: Lee (2018) reports that weekly journal writing in action research helped pre-service English teachers move from surface reflection to critical analysis while also supporting metacognition and emotional expression. Self-study, supported by portfolios and critical friends, allows teachers to integrate personal and professional identities while fostering agency (Bass et al., 2002). Attard (2020) extends this view, arguing that self-study not only deepens educators' own development but also models reflection for their students. Meanwhile, Zwozdiak-Myers (2024) underscores that systematic classroom research turns teachers into connoisseurs and critics of practice, producing new professional knowledge through cycles of planning, acting, observing, and reflecting. Such methodologies reinforce the argument that reflective practice in teacher research is multifaceted, offering diverse yet complementary routes for professional growth.

Reflective practice within teacher research is increasingly framed as both a developmental disposition and an evidence-based enterprise. Farrell (2020) insists that teachers must cultivate a disposition to inquiry, grounded in Dewey's (1933) triad of open-mindedness, responsibility, and wholeheartedness, and to engage meaningfully in Schön's (1983) reflection-in-action, reflection-on-action, and reflection-for-action. Teachers' reflective practice must also be supported by evidence – through systematic data collection from themselves, students, and colleagues – so that they can articulate not only what they do but also why and with what impact (Farrell, 2020). Video-based reflective practice can provide such evidence as it deepens teachers' learning by providing multimodal opportunities to analyse and re-analyse their teaching (Yuan et al., 2020). Likewise, Hartmann et al. (2021) reveal that teachers' ability to integrate multiple sources of information is closely tied to their epistemic reflexivity, underscoring the intellectual demands of reflection. Together, these perspectives indicate that reflective practice in teacher research is at once ethical, intellectual, and methodological; it is anchored in evidence, yet expansive in its forms and possibilities.

Teacher research provides fertile ground for cultivating reflection, whether through action research, exploratory practice, self-study, or other forms of practitioner inquiry. At the same time, recent advances in digital technology are reshaping how teachers collect evidence, analyse their practice, and sustain inquiry. It is in this context that AI emerges as a new partner in teacher reflection.

AI AND TEACHER REFLECTION

Professional development programmes are increasingly using AI to scaffold reflective practice, especially in language education. For instance, a programme grounded in Bandura's (1997) social cognitive theory helped Taiwanese primary teachers integrate AI into English speaking instruction (Yang et al., 2024).

Through iterative cycles of lesson planning, teaching, and reflection, supported by mentoring and an AI speech tool, teachers moved from technical challenges and learner difficulties towards building enactive mastery experiences. This process strengthened their self-efficacy not only in using AI tools but also in managing classrooms, engaging students, and refining instructional strategies. Similarly, Seo et al. (2025) show that teachers envision AI as a complementary partner, one that can assist with curriculum design, instructional materials, evaluation, and even self-reflection. Participants stressed that AI should augment rather than replace their professional autonomy, supporting their work as augmented teachers (Seo et al., 2025). Hence, what is being highlighted is the dual potential of AI: to strengthen teacher confidence through reflective cycles and to extend professional capacity while preserving human agency.

AI can also reshape the kinds of feedback teachers receive during training, thereby broadening reflection. In their comparison of feedback modes, Wang et al. (2025) found that combining observation-based feedback with AI-driven teaching analytics significantly expanded the scope of pre-service teachers' reflections and improved their perceptions of feedback quality, even if short-term teaching performance did not increase. Further evidence comes from a study of Swedish pre-service teachers using QBot, an AI-driven question detection tool (Sert, 2025). Participants reported that the system enhanced their noticing of classroom questioning patterns and supported both reflection-on-action and reflection-for-action. At the same time, they cautioned that human dialogue remains irreplaceable, underscoring the value of AI–human partnerships over AI-only reflection. The suggestion here is that hybrid feedback models that blend human and AI inputs are most effective for fostering reflective practice in teacher education.

Beyond feedback, AI is also being used to provide structured environments for systematic reflection at scale. Phillips (2024) identifies three affordances of AI dashboards for university teachers' reflective practice: they shift reflection towards more objective, action-oriented conclusions, allow flexible natural language queries of student data, and simulate teacher-like monitoring in online contexts. At the same time, these affordances raise concerns about trust, privacy, and equity. In a similar vein, Cai et al. (2025) piloted an AI-powered dashboard with Chinese pre-service teachers and found that it fostered more exploratory and critical discourse than control groups, with participants moving from simple information-sharing to evidence-based reasoning. Zhang (2024) also demonstrates the value of AI feedback systems in fostering teachers' reflective writing, though she stresses the importance of transparency and explainability. These studies reveal that dashboards and feedback tools can deepen reflection if carefully designed, but their ethical dimensions cannot be overlooked.

AI is also being leveraged to support evidence-based reflection through analytics frameworks and toolkits. For example, the TESTII framework, an AI-supported model for classroom teaching analysis and improvement, generates interpretable visual reports of classroom events and co-develops strategies with teachers (Sun et al., 2023). This model aims to move reflection beyond descriptive coding into actionable improvement. Similarly, Phillips et al. (2023) created an AI toolkit that analyses assessment data and lesson transcripts to predict difficult content areas and align them with student performance. Their findings show that such systems reduce the burden of data collection and analysis, allowing both novice and experienced teachers to sustain continuous, evidence-based reflection. Such innovations underscore AI's potential not just as a reflective aid, but as a catalyst for rethinking teacher identity and professional knowledge in an AI-mediated educational landscape (Xerri & Block, 2024, 2025; Xerri et al., 2026). The technology is compelling educators to reimagine themselves as reflective, technologically literate professionals (Ghiasvand & Seyri, 2025).

While the above studies underline the potential of AI to scaffold, broaden, and systematise reflection, they largely focus on analytic or feedback-driven applications. A growing body of work, however, highlights how generative AI tools such as ChatGPT can move beyond analytics to act as co-participants in inquiry and reflective dialogue. The next section explores this emerging partnership.

GENERATIVE AI AS A REFLECTIVE PARTNER

Generative AI is increasingly framed as a catalyst for critical literacy and reflective learning. Experiential, analytical, and reflective activities with AI can help people overcome fear, develop prompting skills (Xerri, 2024), and interrogate stereotypes embedded in outputs (Hu, 2025). Reflection is central here: people learn not only how to use AI but also how to question its communicative patterns and biases. For such a purpose, Meng et al. (2025) designed the RSCQA approach (Reflection, Situation, Complication, Question, Answer), which is meant to enhance pre-service teachers' AI literacy and critical thinking, with the latter component being vital for the success of the former (Xerri, 2025b). Their study shows that structured reflection pushes educators beyond surface engagement into higher-order reasoning. Nguyen and Nguyen (2025) reinforce this point in design tasks, where participants who engaged in iterative reflection produced stronger outcomes than those who passively adopted AI suggestions. Likewise, Liu et al. (2025) show that teachers' self-efficacy with generative AI, combined with reflective practice, significantly predicts students' English achievement, underscoring the dual importance of confidence and reflection for effective AI integration in language education. One key idea that can be distilled from these findings is that reflection provides the bridge between AI's affordances and authentic professional learning, transforming AI from a tool into a partner in critical engagement.

Reflection with AI has also proven transformative in teacher education, where it supports both pedagogical design and professional identity. Jou et al. (2025) show that pre-service vocational teachers developed confidence and situated Technological Pedagogical Content Knowledge as they reflected on ethical and practical issues while designing with AI. In-service teachers have similarly benefitted: Yeh (2025) documents how inquiry-based learning projects supported by ChatGPT enabled teachers to design creative lessons, microteach, and reflect collaboratively on pedagogy. Zhao et al. (2025) extend this view by showing how lesson study cycles enabled EFL teachers to move from passive use of AI-generated resources to active refinement and strategic collaboration, with reflective discussions catalysing professional growth. These accounts indicate that AI, when coupled with systematic reflection, not only supports lesson planning but also reshapes teachers' agency and pedagogical reasoning.

Teacher educators are also using AI to spark reflection on wider issues of pedagogy, assessment, and ethics. Estaiteyeh and McQuirter (2024) describe workshops where educators critically examined both the opportunities and risks of AI integration, ranging from personalisation to plagiarism. Busuttil (2024) adds that ChatGPT can enhance reflective lesson planning within an Assessment as Learning framework, though limitations in inclusivity and clarity remain. Similarly, AI can foster active learning by supporting metacognition and reflective practice, encouraging individuals to critically assess strategies while engaging in deeper problem-solving (ElSayary, 2024). However, overreliance on AI can erode teacher agency, diminishing decisiveness and self-reflection (Phan & Trinh, 2025). Teachers can resist this problematic tendency by distributing roles between themselves and AI, refining questioning skills, and maintaining offline practices (Phan & Trinh, 2025). Thus, reflection is essential in ensuring AI integration strengthens rather than undermines teacher professionalism.

Collaboration between teachers and AI is increasingly conceptualised as a form of reflective partnership, though its boundaries remain contested. Outamgharte et al. (2025) report that Moroccan EFL teachers valued AI for feedback and idea generation but emphasised that it cannot replace human dialogue in reflection. Arefian et al. (2024) further show how ChatGPT functioned as a mentor and reflective peer, while communities of practice humanised and contextualised its feedback. At the same time, Lim and Nicolaides (2024) situate AI within a broader epistemological shift, arguing that tools like ChatGPT disrupt traditional notions of certainty and mastery and demand what they call 'generative knowing', a reflective stance that embraces uncertainty and relational ethics. This shift reframes reflective practice as more-than-human, where AI becomes part of the dialogic process but not its sole arbiter. These insights suggest that effective teacher–AI collaboration depends on educators' ability to critically evaluate AI's contributions while maintaining human judgement and ethical responsibility.

Finally, AI-enhanced reflective tools are beginning to reshape classroom observation and storytelling practices. Wei et al. (2025) show that AI-assisted digital storytelling promotes multidimensional reflection, encouraging pre-service teachers to consider problems, solutions, and contextual factors across single-, double-, and triple-loop levels. Lee et al. (2024) present VidAAS, a GPT-4 Vision–based system that provides teachers with accurate classroom analytics for both real-time and post-lesson reflection. While promising, teachers who used the system noted the need to balance AI-driven data with qualitative human insight, particularly around privacy. Such research demonstrates that generative AI is not simply a content generator but a reflective partner, capable of prompting, structuring, and extending professional learning, provided its integration is guided by critical evaluation, human judgement, and ethical awareness.

Taken as a whole, the above findings illustrate how generative AI is transforming reflective practice: providing teachers with new ways to analyse their pedagogy, co-construct knowledge, and reimagine professional identity. As such, it challenges teacher-researchers to consider how reflection in the age of AI can be facilitated responsibly, critically, and creatively.

FACILITATING REFLECTION ON CLASSROOM INQUIRY WITH GENERATIVE AI

Generative AI offers distinctive affordances for teacher-researchers by acting as a scaffold, co-analyst, and dialogic partner in reflection. While reflective practice remains central to teacher learning (Farrell, 2016; Marshall et al., 2022), its enactment is often constrained by time, cognitive load, and access to peers. AI can ease these constraints by generating prompts, offering alternative perspectives, and structuring feedback. Conceptually, this positions AI as more than an efficiency tool: it is a co-participant that stimulates questioning and supports analysis. This view resonates with Lim and Nicolaides' (2024) idea of generative knowing, which reframes reflection as an open-ended engagement with uncertainty, and aligns with exploratory practice's emphasis on teachers investigating classroom puzzles (Miller et al., 2021).

AI can be integrated across different models of teacher research. Within lesson study, for example, it can support planning by suggesting task variations or mapping objectives onto Bloom's taxonomy (Busuttil, 2024), while video-based analysis and AI-generated prompts enable teachers to interrogate transcripts and feedback patterns in post-lesson reflection (Sert, 2025; Yuan et al., 2020). Similarly, in action research cycles, AI can aid planning by surfacing misconceptions and suggesting strategies (Apelgren et al., 2015), support classroom action with adaptive questioning prompts, assist observation through pattern detection in transcripts or field notes (Wang et al., 2025), and generate reflective prompts that push analysis through multiple lenses (Cornish, 2024). These integrations make inquiry more feasible and help practitioners move from descriptive accounts to critical, transformative reflection (Maxwell, 2024; Soomro, 2018).

Generative AI also holds potential for co-analysis of data. Teacher-researchers often struggle with the volume and complexity of classroom evidence, from journals to video transcripts. AI tools can highlight emergent themes, detect patterns in questioning or interaction, and compare observed practices to theoretical frameworks. Yet the critical step remains human interpretation: AI suggestions should function as provocations that broaden inquiry rather than definitive judgements. In this sense, AI mirrors the role of a critical friend (Arefian et al., 2024), offering challenge and perspective that teachers then contextualise and humanise within their communities of practice (Dana & Yendol-Hoppey, 2010).

At the same time, teacher-researchers must remain alert to challenges. Overreliance on AI risks undermining teacher agency and reflective judgement (Phan & Trinh, 2025), and ethical questions arise around data privacy (Phillips, 2024), algorithmic bias (Hu, 2025), and the erosion of human interaction in reflective dialogue (Outamgharte et al., 2025). Thus, integrating AI into classroom inquiry requires a stance of critical partnership, one where teachers retain ownership of reflection, deliberately balance AI-generated insights with human interpretation, and treat AI outputs as one voice among many in inquiry.

Building on these insights, the RPF is proposed to guide teacher-researchers in productively working with generative AI (see Figure 2.1).

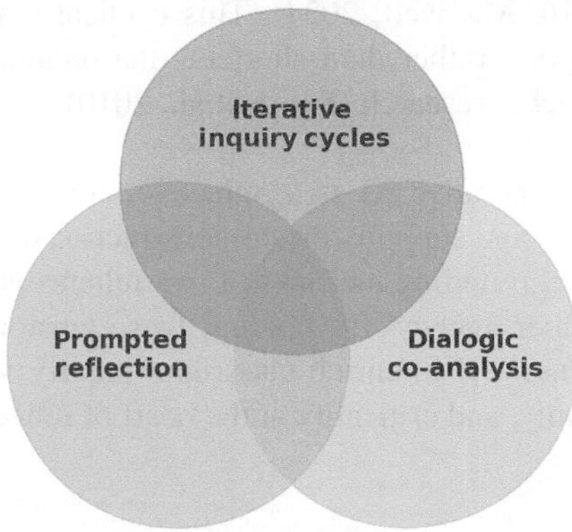

FIGURE 2.1 Reflective partnership framework.

The framework comprises three interrelated dimensions:

1. Prompted reflection: Teacher-researchers can use generative AI to formulate reflective questions tailored to classroom puzzles or problems. For example, after a lesson, teachers might ask an AI tool to provide critical prompts aligned with Brookfield's (2017) lenses, encouraging them to consider student perspectives, theoretical insights, and wider institutional contexts. This creates structured triggers that move reflection beyond descriptive recall (Marshall et al., 2021; Senese, 2017).
2. Dialogic co-analysis: Generative AI can support the analysis of classroom data (transcripts, lesson plans, or journals) by highlighting patterns and offering alternative interpretations. Such co-analysis can broaden the scope of teachers' noticing, while maintaining human judgement as the ultimate arbiter. Teacher-researchers can thus engage in reflection in partnership with AI, while also discussing AI-generated insights with peers to preserve the relational dimension highlighted by Marshall et al. (2022).
3. Iterative inquiry cycles: Just as action research relies on planning, acting, observing, and reflecting (Cabaroglu, 2015), generative AI can be embedded across some of these stages with further support being provided by other AI tools. During planning, generative AI might suggest lesson variations; during action, AI-powered tools can provide immediate analytics; during observation, AI can support multimodal analysis; and during reflection, generative AI can scaffold multiple levels of criticality, from technical to transformative

(Farrell, 2016; Maxwell, 2024). This cyclical embedding ensures that AI supports rather than shortcuts the ongoing inquiry stance central to teacher research (Smith et al., 2010).

The RPF positions generative AI as a reflective partner that scaffolds noticing, broadens inquiry, and supports the co-construction of professional knowledge, while also foregrounding the risks of overreliance, ethical compromise, and erosion of teacher agency. By holding these tensions in view, teacher-researchers can harness AI to enrich classroom inquiry while preserving the autonomy, relationality, and criticality at the heart of reflective practice.

CONCLUSION

This chapter has explored how generative AI can act as a reflective partner for teacher-researchers, enhancing the long-standing traditions of reflective practice and classroom inquiry. It has shown that while reflection is foundational to professional growth, it is often constrained by the demands of teaching, the complexity of classroom evidence, and the challenge of sustaining systematic inquiry. Generative AI offers promising affordances that can help overcome these barriers without displacing teacher agency (Xerri, 2025a).

The RPF encapsulates these possibilities by outlining three interrelated dimensions – prompted reflection, dialogic co-analysis, and iterative inquiry cycles – that together position AI as a scaffold, collaborator, and stimulus for deeper professional learning. Through these dimensions, AI becomes less a tool of efficiency and more a partner in cultivating criticality, creativity, and sustained inquiry. This chapter has also stressed the need for balance: while AI can broaden perspectives and surface new insights, its outputs must be contextualised through human judgement, ethical reflection, and collaborative dialogue.

The future of reflective practice in teacher research therefore lies not in choosing between human or machine insight, but in forging partnerships that preserve the relational, critical, and ethical core of reflection while harnessing the affordances of new technologies. Generative AI can enrich teachers' professional lives by easing cognitive burdens, amplifying inquiry, and supporting the co-construction of pedagogical knowledge. Yet its integration must remain guided by principles of autonomy, equity, and responsibility. By adopting a critical and creative stance towards generative AI, teacher-researchers can sustain reflection as a transformative practice, one that bridges research and pedagogy, strengthens teacher identity, and reimagines professional growth for the age of AI.

Using ChatGPT in Management Research 3

A Practical Guide for Scholars

INTRODUCTION

The release of ChatGPT to the public in November 2022 was a resounding success as illustrated by the quick and high adoption by around 100 million users (Paris, 2023), significant media attention (e.g., Dodd, 2023; *The Economist*, 2023; Weed, 2023), and the development of new businesses and business models based on ChatGPT (Chui et al., 2022; James, 2023). Unsurprisingly, many management researchers have begun exploring the potential of ChatGPT for their studies, articles, book chapters, teaching, data analysis, and dissertations (Dwivedi et al., 2023; Sheetal et al., 2023). In one extreme example, a recent article even listed ChatGPT as a co-author (Kung et al., 2023). This approach has since been widely criticised, because AI tools do not meet common authorship criteria (e.g., accountability, intellectual contribution, and responsibility for the work). Instead, publishers require transparent disclosure of their use in the methods and/or acknowledgements sections. The introduction of ChatGPT has brought about a myriad of possibilities for the management research landscape. With its cutting-edge features, ChatGPT has the power to revolutionise the way research is conducted. However, as with any new technology, it is crucial to explore and address the critical questions raised about its impact on research.

DOI: 10.1201/9781003786405-4

One of the key questions is whether ChatGPT will truly facilitate empirical studies and the research process, as other groundbreaking technologies have done in the past decades. This question is not without precedent; it echoes the transformative effects of past technological milestones. Will ChatGPT follow in the footsteps of other revolutionary technologies, such as the development of the internet, statistical data analysis software, qualitative data analysis tools, online search engines, databases, and reference management programmes? These innovations have shaped research in recent decades, and the challenge now is to determine if ChatGPT will contribute similarly, fostering new methodologies and expanding the boundaries of what is possible in management research.

In contrast, some researchers believe that its use could have detrimental consequences on management research. It could, for instance, encourage deception and cheating, reduce creativity, lead to standardised research outputs, and potentially make some research jobs obsolete. It is essential to proceed with caution and carefully consider the potential risks and downsides of ChatGPT. Researchers should avoid relying too heavily on the technology and neglecting other important aspects of the research process, such as critical thinking and creativity. There seems to be a risk that ChatGPT could lead to a homogenisation of research outputs, as many researchers begin to use the same tools and approaches.

This chapter addresses these concerns to fully exploit the potential of the use of ChatGPT in management research and avoid its pitfalls. In doing so, it makes several contributions. First, this chapter offers a step-by-step plan for using ChatGPT in management research to guide researchers, students, and practitioners. This chapter can be a valuable resource for those interested in using ChatGPT in their research or for instructors teaching research methods classes and workshops at universities and research organisations. Second, this chapter explains which research tasks are suitable for ChatGPT and which are not. Third, this chapter discusses practical challenges in using ChatGPT and ways to overcome them. Finally, this chapter suggests avenues for future research and how future studies can integrate ChatGPT effectively.

METHODOLOGICAL APPROACH

ChatGPT

ChatGPT is an AI language model that uses natural language processing to provide researchers with answers to their questions from a wide range of domains. ChatGPT is based on inputted data from the internet and can generate answers to complex questions, provide information and recommendations, and solve complex problems. Users can engage in a conversation with ChatGPT and follow up on their questions. ChatGPT also allows users to upload documents, create images and diagrams, and conduct calculations and analyses. In March 2023, OpenAI introduced ChatGPT version 4 and offered the possibility to subscribe to ChatGPT Plus, which provides faster and more frequent responses than the free version. In August 2025, OpenAI released version 5.

Interview with ChatGPT

This chapter used a structured interview with ChatGPT 4.0. To structure this chapter and develop the interview questions and topics, previous work about best practices for management research was consulted (Adamovic, 2020; Aguinis & Bradley, 2014; Brewis, 2014; Clancy & Vince, 2019; Dunwoodie et al., 2023; Dwivedi et al., 2023; Fisher et al., 2023; Sheng et al., 2021). In particular, several handbooks of management research methods (Bell et al., 2022; Saunders et al., 2019; Schindler, 2021) were used as a guide for the interview questions. Based on these books, the interview questions about the use of ChatGPT in management research were grouped into eight categories: 1) academic writing, 2) research topic, 3) literature review, 4) theory, 5) research model and hypotheses, 6) research design, 7) data analysis, and 8) discussion section. For each category, several questions were about the best way of using ChatGPT for specific research tasks, as well as about the disadvantages of using ChatGPT for these research tasks. To summarise and synthesise the interview responses, 8 overall categories will be used, and advantages and disadvantages will be discussed for each category. The interview questions are presented at the end of this chapter.

Asking the Right Questions

According to its website description, it is essential to be detailed and precise when preparing questions for ChatGPT (OpenAI, 2022). The questions for ChatGPT are often called prompts, and developing the right questions or adapting the questions for better answers is called prompt engineering. The absence of face-to-face communication makes communication with ChatGPT prone to misunderstandings. However, if ChatGPT misunderstands a question, it is essential to ask the same question in a more detailed and precise way. It could also help to provide more information about the context, rephrase the question, or use different terms to obtain a helpful answer. Relatedly, suppose ChatGPT states that it does not know the answer to a question or has no access to the requested information. In that case, users can continue by asking their question differently or indirectly to obtain a helpful answer from ChatGPT.

INTERVIEW FINDINGS

In this section, ChatGPT's interview responses are synthesised in eight categories based on the frameworks present in handbooks about management research methods (Bell et al., 2022; Saunders et al., 2019; Schindler, 2021): 1) academic writing, 2) research topic, 3) literature review, 4) theory, 5) research model and hypotheses, 6) research design, 7) data analysis, and 8) discussion section. For each category, this chapter discusses which research tasks ChatGPT can be used for and which ones it should not be used for (see Table 3.1 for an overview). This information will enable management researchers to evaluate whether ChatGPT is the right tool for their research.

TABLE 3.1 Strengths and limitations of ChatGPT for management research tasks

TASK	*CHATGPT'S STRENGTHS*	*CHATGPT'S LIMITATIONS*
Academic writing	proofreading, editing, tightening up arguments, formal and academic language	highly specialised and technical language, formatting, style, logical and critical argumentation, copyright issues, and text outputs require proofreading
Research topic	generating ideas and topics, refining a topic, developing research questions, ideas for a research proposal and an introduction	critical evaluation of ideas, creativity, originality, does not know a researcher's background and strengths, knowledge exchange with colleagues cannot be simulated, well-structured and coherent writing, identifying research gaps, explaining the importance of the topic, identifying the contributions, integrating the research context

(*Continued*)

TABLE 3.1 (Continued)

TASK	*CHATGPT'S STRENGTHS*	*CHATGPT'S LIMITATIONS*
Literature review	summarising prior research, identifying essential studies, summaries of individual articles and books, synthesising articles for a general summary of a research stream, strengths and weaknesses of previous studies, future research directions, drawing lessons from other research areas	evaluate the quality of studies, sometimes lacks access to articles behind publisher paywalls, sometimes has wrong references
Theory	an overview of theories and frameworks used in the past, definitions and summaries of theories and frameworks	generic responses, non-integration of research context, critical thinking, addressing counterarguments, evaluating the fit of theory with the research questions, and developing a new theory
Research model and hypotheses	propose variables that address research questions and are consistent with the theory, propose relationships between variables and hypotheses	novelty of model, evaluation of ideas, logical and consistent argumentation, consideration of research context
Research design	advice regarding research approach and different designs, structure and question format for survey, propose open-ended interview questions, examples of questions of previous studies, anonymisation, confidentiality, and informed consent forms, sampling techniques	evaluating the feasibility and rigour of a study design, measurement scales are often incorrect, integrating research context, adapting questions to interview participants, assessing the importance of different ethical concerns, knowing specific requirements and procedures regarding ethics applications at different universities, and tailoring sampling designs

(*Continued*)

TABLE 3.1 (Continued)

TASK	*CHATGPT'S STRENGTHS*	*CHATGPT'S LIMITATIONS*
Data analysis	recommendations for data management, suggest data analysis techniques, strengths/weaknesses and assumptions/limitations of data analysis techniques and statistical tests, using Python	conducting statistical analyses, complex and advanced statistical analyses, using software packages for advanced analyses (Mplus, SPSS, Stata, R, etc.), cleaning and organising complex datasets, critical evaluation and interpretation of the outputs
Discussion section	suggest several general ideas for contributions and practical implications, summarise a study's key contributions, and propose how the study's contributions relate to past research	nuanced recommendations specific to the study and its context, detailed and critical evaluation of the study's contributions, evaluation of a researcher's own research and how it fits within a larger research stream, critical analysis of a study's limitations and strengths, and detailed future research directions based on the study

Academic Writing

ChatGPT can be a valuable tool for improving the writing of academic articles, books, and dissertations (Stokel-Walker & Van Noorden, 2023; van Dis et al., 2023). For example, to improve their writing, researchers can use ChatGPT as their coach and ask for feedback about their writing. Researchers can also copy and paste their text into ChatGPT and ask it to proofread the text, correct any grammatical mistakes, and clarify the language. Researchers should be as specific as possible and instruct ChatGPT whether it should check for grammar, punctuation, or syntax. ChatGPT also offers more advanced possibilities, such as tightening up arguments and rewriting text more formally and academically (Kasneci et al., 2023). ChatGPT can also simplify language when the text is overly complex or technical. For non-native speakers, these options could be a game-changer, saving them time and energy. ChatGPT could also save non-native speakers financial resources by providing a free alternative to expensive editing services that publishers offer. As an alternative to ChatGPT, researchers can also use other cloud-based typing and writing assistants, such as Grammarly and Hemingway Editor.

Despite the potential benefits of ChatGPT for academic writing, researchers should be careful when using it for this task. Although ChatGPT can proofread and edit text sections, it occasionally makes mistakes. Researchers should therefore double-check all sections that ChatGPT has edited. Relatedly, ChatGPT could have issues with highly specialised and technical language in management research.

It is important to note, from a research conduct perspective, that authors of manuscripts should limit the use of ChatGPT to proofreading and editing and not trust it to engage in critical thinking and evaluation of their arguments. Providing logical and critical argumentation or addressing potential counterarguments are not strengths of ChatGPT, and responsibility for these core scholarly tasks remains with the researcher. While researchers can use ChatGPT for proofreading and editing, they should not copy and paste text outputs generated from scratch, as this could raise concerns related to copyright and authorship. ChatGPT can generate new and creative text outputs, which may reduce the risk of conventional plagiarism. However, its training data could include copyrighted material, meaning that copying and pasting text may still create copyright issues. Reputable publishers also require authors to write their own text as part of responsible research practice. While fair use rules and guidelines may apply to non-commercial research and scholarship, it remains crucial to be mindful of copyright and authorship issues when using ChatGPT.

Research Topic

A strength of ChatGPT in the research process is its ability to support researchers in brainstorming and generating ideas and topics for their studies. Researchers can provide a general topic of interest and ask ChatGPT for potential research ideas. However, it is the researcher's responsibility to evaluate these ideas and determine which are original and important to investigate. An excellent understanding of the relevant literature is also essential to identify which topics have already been investigated and which require empirical research. Importantly, researchers should select their own research topic and not ChatGPT. ChatGPT does not know a researcher's skills, knowledge, interests, work experience, strengths, weaknesses, hobbies, etc. Selecting the right topic also requires a good fit to the researcher's expertise and interests.

Once the researcher has selected a topic, ChatGPT can help refine it and develop more specific research questions. After having developed their starting research questions, researchers can ask ChatGPT to create more detailed sub-questions. Nevertheless, researchers should not neglect to engage in discussions with colleagues and present their work at conferences. ChatGPT cannot yet replace the collaborative knowledge and information exchange among colleagues, which often leads to creative and innovative ideas.

As a next step, ChatGPT can provide researchers with ideas on the outline of a research proposal, how to structure it, and which topics to include. Similarly, ChatGPT can also offer ideas and suggestions for the introduction section. However, it is essential to state that researchers should write their own proposal and introduction. While ChatGPT can provide ideas, it may not have the same capability as a top researcher and writer to write a coherent, well-structured, and critical proposal and introduction. However, it may still be a useful tool for early-career researchers (e.g., helping them generate initial ideas, improving clarity and structure, or refining language). ChatGPT's strengths do not lie in critical thinking, identifying research gaps, explaining the importance of the topic, identifying the contributions, and integrating the research context. Finally, researchers can ask ChatGPT to propose engaging titles for their article.

Literature Review

One practical application of ChatGPT for management researchers is in the starting process of a literature review, such as narrative or scoping reviews, or for the preparatory phase of systematic reviews. ChatGPT can summarise previous research on a topic and identify essential studies in the field. It can provide summaries of individual articles and books, synthesising them to give a general overview of a research stream. ChatGPT can also provide general guidance on the strengths and weaknesses of previous studies, as well as areas for future research improvement. ChatGPT can also propose keywords for an effective literature search and list several key authors in a research area. Interestingly, ChatGPT can draw lessons from other research areas, creating a basis for interdisciplinary research projects. However, researchers must determine on their own how valuable these lessons are for their own research project and field.

Despite the potential benefits, researchers need to be cautious when using ChatGPT for their literature review. While it can offer general guidance on research gaps and strengths and weaknesses of previous research, it cannot evaluate well the quality of individual studies in terms of the reliability and originality of research methods, data analysis, and contributions. Instead, researchers need to conduct this critical evaluation themselves. This also means that ChatGPT is less useful for systematic literature reviews that require a detailed and rigorous search process. Additionally, ChatGPT may struggle to summarise and synthesise highly technical and emerging research areas in management research. It also sometimes has no access to academic journals that require a subscription. This could be a significant issue for fast-moving research fields. Other researchers may have already addressed potential research gaps identified by ChatGPT in recent months or years.

Another issue with the literature review process is that ChatGPT occasionally provides incorrect references or non-academic references in its responses to user questions. This means users do not know which sources ChatGPT has used to create the text output or whether the sources are credible. To avoid this issue, users can ask ChatGPT to list its sources and to include in-text citations. However, users should still double-check the references that ChatGPT provides.

Theory

An essential step in most research projects is to select an appropriate theory or framework to choose variables for the research model, explain the hypotheses, and guide the study design (Bell et al., 2022; Saunders et al., 2019; Schindler, 2021). ChatGPT can provide researchers with general information on the theories and frameworks used in past research related to a specific topic. This can give researchers a good overview of which theories are available, and which ones may fit well with their topic and research question. Researchers can also request definitions and research summaries of specific theories or frameworks.

However, researchers must provide ChatGPT with detailed information about their research questions, topics, objectives, ideas, and context. Otherwise, the responses will be too general. For example, asking ChatGPT about theories related to organisational behaviour, leadership, innovation management, human resource management, or team management will lead to a response that includes many theories without considering the specific context and research questions.

Importantly, researchers should not rely on ChatGPT to select the theory for them but use the information that it provides to select a theory on their own. Selecting a theory involves critical thinking, addressing counterarguments, and evaluating the fit with the research questions and context. All these tasks still require human researchers. Relatedly, while ChatGPT can provide an overview of theories used in past research on a topic, it is not yet suitable for developing a new theory. Instead, researchers should conduct qualitative research studies and critically engage with the literature. Discussing their ideas with colleagues is also an essential element in the development of a new theory.

Research Model and Hypotheses

For quantitative researchers, it is often essential to develop a research model and hypotheses to test in their empirical study. ChatGPT can assist in the selection of key variables for the research model. Researchers can ask ChatGPT to propose variables that address their research questions and objectives and are consistent with the theory or framework they have selected. To facilitate communication with ChatGPT, researchers should have already developed their research questions and objectives, conducted a literature review, and selected an overall theory or framework. Providing this information to ChatGPT can improve the quality of its suggestions.

ChatGPT can also be used to propose relationships among the variables of a research model. Management researchers may ask ChatGPT to generate ideas for more sophisticated models, including mediating variables (e.g., mechanisms that explain underlying psychological processes) and moderating variables (e.g., boundary conditions or contextual influences). However, getting helpful ideas for complex research models often requires follow-up questions from the researcher that are detailed and precise. Asking such questions requires the researcher to have an excellent knowledge of the literature and past research. In addition, researchers should select the variables of their research model themselves. It is necessary that researchers critically evaluate ChatGPT's propositions to analyse if they make sense and provide a novel contribution. While ChatGPT is useful for generating ideas, it is less effective at assessing their quality. Researchers should stay up to date on the most recent research in their field.

Building on the research model, ChatGPT can propose hypotheses to explain the relationships between the variables. It can also suggest theories and arguments to explain the hypotheses and propose previous studies that align with the theoretical ideas. Nevertheless, researchers should write the hypotheses themselves, as ChatGPT has limited capability to provide a logical and consistent argumentation or evaluate whether the hypotheses make sense in a specific research context.

ChatGPT can also act as an academic reviewer to provide critical feedback. Therefore, researchers can ask ChatGPT to play the devil's advocate as an academic peer reviewer and provide critical or even negative feedback about their hypotheses. This could help researchers discover any issues with their hypotheses or identify any cofounding variables that they left out of their hypotheses.

Research Design

To design their study, researchers can ask ChatGPT to propose research methods to test their hypotheses and address their research questions. ChatGPT can provide general advice regarding the selection between quantitative, qualitative, and mixed-method research approaches. It can also provide more detailed advice. For example, if a researcher wants to conduct an experimental study, ChatGPT can differentiate between experimental, field experimental, quasi-experimental, and non-experimental designs. However, researchers should make their own decisions and use ChatGPT only as a tool to inform their decision-making. ChatGPT cannot evaluate the feasibility of a study or the rigour of a research design. To ensure a high-quality research design, researchers need to be experts in the respective research method and discuss with their colleagues.

ChatGPT can further help researchers to prepare questions for their survey and interview studies. For survey development, it can suggest the structure of the survey, question format, and measurement scales. However, the measurement scales it provides are often incorrect (different from the original measurement items) and should not be used by researchers. Instead, researchers need to be well familiar with existing measurement approaches in their research field or develop and test new measurement scales.

ChatGPT can be useful for addressing ethical concerns during the study, such as anonymisation, confidentiality, and informed consent forms. It can also provide researchers with ideas and recommendations on which topics and arguments to include in their ethics application. However, ChatGPT cannot evaluate the importance of different ethical concerns and procedures or know the specific requirements and procedures regarding ethics applications at various universities.

ChatGPT can provide general advice about sampling techniques, such as cluster sampling, stratified sampling, snowball sampling, convenience sampling, simple random sampling, and systematic sampling. This can help researchers to think about an appropriate sampling technique for their study. However, researchers should be aware that ChatGPT cannot provide tailored sampling designs that are often required in empirical studies. ChatGPT further provides recommendations about the selection of the target population and the necessary level of heterogeneity, as well as suggestions about how to get research access. Nonetheless, the researcher must still negotiate research access with organisations, schedule and conduct interviews, distribute surveys, access company datasets, and so on. That said, researchers can ask ChatGPT to help with this process. For example, they could instruct ChatGPT to prepare emails for organisations, inviting them to engage in collaboration.

Data Analysis

ChatGPT can propose recommendations for data management, such as cleaning the data, managing missing data, and handling outliers. Additionally, ChatGPT can suggest which data analysis technique the researcher could use to analyse the data. It can provide an overview of the strengths and weaknesses, as well as the assumptions and limitations, of different data analysis techniques and statistical tests. ChatGPT can also help to identify potential mistakes in a syntax (e.g., SPSS, Mplus, and R syntaxes). While ChatGPT is a good starting point for data analysis, researchers must have an excellent knowledge of statistics and data analysis techniques to select the proper technique and statistical test.

ChatGPT can conduct statistical analyses using Python. However, researchers should not rely solely on the results of the statistical analyses provided by ChatGPT, as mistakes can occur, especially when it runs highly complex and advanced statistical analyses. Researchers must conduct the analyses on their own using Python or a statistical software package for advanced analyses (Mplus, SPSS, Stata, R, etc.). Although ChatGPT can access online datasets, it struggles to clean and organise complex datasets. If researchers provide ChatGPT with access to their data, they must anonymise the data and have permission to share it with ChatGPT. Relatedly, if ChatGPT provides confidential or sensitive information in its responses, researchers must anonymise the responses before publishing or communicating them. ChatGPT can further offer suggestions for interpreting the statistical output, but researchers must conduct the critical evaluation and interpretation of the outputs themselves. Finally, ChatGPT can provide recommendations on how to visualise the results and how to write them up.

Discussion Section of a Manuscript

ChatGPT can be a helpful starting point for the discussion section of a study by generating general ideas and recommendations. However, it cannot provide more nuanced and tailored recommendations specific to the study and its context. For the theoretical contribution section, ChatGPT can summarise the study's key contributions and propose how these relate to previous research and theories. However, it cannot provide a detailed and critical evaluation of the study's contributions. It also lacks access to research published behind a paywall. Using ChatGPT may also limit researchers from integrating their own expertise and experience in the discussion section. The discussion section is an excellent opportunity for researchers to evaluate their own research and how it fits within a larger research stream.

Regarding the practical implications section, ChatGPT can suggest several general ideas about how practitioners and organisations can apply the study's findings, and what potential policy implications are. However, researchers must critically evaluate these ideas and decide if they make sense in their study's context. Similarly, ChatGPT can generate general ideas about the study's limitations, strengths, future research avenues, and conclusions. Still, it is up to the researcher to provide a more detailed and nuanced critical analysis of the study's limitations and strengths and how future research can expand on the study's conclusions. It could help to ask for more specific questions. For example, instead of asking for the study's general limitations and strengths, researchers could ask for particular limitations and strengths related to the study's design, methodology, or data analysis.

DISCUSSION

ChatGPT can be an efficient, supportive, and convenient research tool that can facilitate the research process for management researchers. Therefore, publishers and educational institutions should not forbid the use of ChatGPT but discuss how to best integrate it into the research process. However, ChatGPT should not be used for all research tasks in management research. To fully exploit the potential of ChatGPT in management research, this chapter presented a guide for using ChatGPT. While ChatGPT can provide general advice and be helpful in proofreading, summarising previous research, generating research ideas, and providing ideas for a study design, ChatGPT is sometimes less useful for specific advice and for data analysis, critical thinking and evaluation, creativity and originality, and identifying literature sources and references.

Future research can build on this chapter to use ChatGPT in an effective way to facilitate, improve, and speed up the research process. The use of ChatGPT can enhance the quality and quantity of researchers' outputs. It can also help non-native speakers improve the quality of their writing, enabling them to publish their work in prestigious journals, which often require a high level of English skills. Although the use of ChatGPT can improve the quality of research outputs, researchers must not neglect their own skills, knowledge, and abilities. They must integrate their expertise and knowledge about previous research and literature, engage in critical thinking and evaluation, be creative and innovative, and work with colleagues to generate high-quality research projects and outputs.

Future research is needed to develop a similar guide for the use of ChatGPT in teaching. While some schools and universities have forbidden the use of ChatGPT (e.g., Nolan, 2023; Williams, 2023), it might be better for educational institutions to embrace new technologies and teach researchers and students how to use them effectively, ethically, and fairly. While their concerns about deception and plagiarism are sometimes justified, universities need to help researchers increase their knowledge about ChatGPT and generative AI. This knowledge is important not only for designing assessments that reduce opportunities for dishonesty, but also for supporting responsible research conduct, including transparent uses of generative AI in research design, analysis, and writing. Furthermore, future research is needed to provide regular updates to this chapter as the development of ChatGPT and related technologies is progressing rapidly, necessitating new insights on integrating generative AI into the research process. Against this background, the present chapter should be understood as an initial and situated contribution, grounded in the authors' perspectives, research and teaching experience, and discussions with colleagues and students, and therefore open to further refinement as the field evolves.

A final issue to consider is the potential for bias arising from ChatGPT's training data. Prior research on the use of AI in organisational and work contexts has documented such biases and their implications (e.g., Cohen, 2019; Houser, 2019; Mirowska & Mesnet, 2022; Shrestha et al., 2019; Tambe et al., 2019; Vassilopoulou et al., 2024). If the training data reflect societal biases, generative AI systems such as ChatGPT may reproduce these biases in their outputs and reinforce existing inequalities if not carefully monitored. Management researchers need to apply a diversity and inclusion lens when using ChatGPT. Future research can also investigate the risk of bias and discrimination when using ChatGPT in management research.

DECLARATION

ChatGPT was employed, and its application is described in detail in the Methods section of this chapter.

INTERVIEW QUESTIONS

1. Introduction:
   Act as an expert in research methods for management research. I kindly request your responses to several questions about the use of ChatGPT. I have prepared a series of interview questions specifically focused on the best practices of utilising ChatGPT in the context of management research. Management research encompasses various areas, such as human resource management, organisational behaviour, organisational research, international management,

strategic management, leadership, operations, change management, technology management, innovation management, and conflict management. Additionally, the US Academy of Management serves as one of the leading academic associations for management research, boasting numerous subdivisions and research areas.

2. Academic writing:
   a) Can you please tell me what is the best way of using ChatGPT in management research for academic writing including proofreading, editing, improving language, tightening up arguments, rewriting text in a more formal way, and rewriting text in a more academic way?
   b) For which tasks related to academic writing (including proofreading, editing, improving language, tightening up arguments, rewriting text in a more formal way, and rewriting text in a more academic way) should management researchers not use ChatGPT?
3. Research topic:
   a) Can you please tell me what is the best way of using ChatGPT in management research for developing a research topic including brainstorming, developing research ideas, choosing a research topic, providing ideas for research questions, providing ideas for a research proposal, providing ideas for an abstract based on a selected research topic, and providing ideas for an introduction based on a selected research topic?
   b) For which tasks related to developing a research topic (including brainstorming, developing research ideas, choosing a research topic, providing ideas for research questions, providing ideas for a research proposal, providing ideas for an abstract based on a selected research topic, and providing ideas for an introduction based on a selected research topic) should management researchers not use ChatGPT?
4. Literature review:
   a) Can you please tell me what is the best way of using ChatGPT in management research for a literature review including summarising previous research (around 1–3 pages), critically reviewing previous research, identifying research gaps, and identifying lessons from past research or related research fields?
   b) For which tasks related to a literature review (including summarising previous research (around 1–3 pages), critically reviewing previous research, identifying research gaps, and identifying lessons from past research or related research fields) should management researchers not use ChatGPT?

5. Theory:
   a) Can you please tell me what is the best way of using ChatGPT in management research for selecting a theory for an empirical study including providing ideas for a theory or theoretical framework for a research topic, research question or research objectives and defining a theory and summarising previous research about the theory?
   b) For which tasks related to selecting a theory or theoretical framework (including providing ideas for a theory or theoretical framework for research topic, research question or research objectives; and defining a theory and summarising previous research about the theory) should management researchers not use ChatGPT?

6. Research model and hypotheses:
   a) Can you please tell me what is the best way of using ChatGPT in management research for developing a research model and hypotheses including providing ideas for a research model; providing ideas for hypotheses; and providing ideas to explain hypotheses by drawing on a theory, logical arguments, and previous research?
   b) For which tasks related to developing a research model and hypotheses (including providing ideas for a research model; providing ideas for hypotheses; and providing ideas to explain hypotheses by drawing on a theory, logical arguments, and previous research) should management researchers not use ChatGPT?

7. Research design:
   a) Can you please tell me what is the best way of using ChatGPT in management research for selecting a research design including providing recommendations for the research design; providing recommendations for research methods; survey design; selecting measurement scales for a survey study; developing ideas for questions for an interview study; preparing an ethics application; providing recommendations for a required sample to test hypotheses or address research questions such as sample characteristics, sample size, type of employees, teams, or organisation; providing recommendations for effective data collection; providing recommendations for research access; and sampling techniques?
   b) For which tasks related to developing a research design (including providing recommendations for the research design; providing recommendations for research methods; survey design; selecting

measurement scales for a survey study; developing ideas for questions for an interview study; preparing an ethics application; providing recommendations for a required sample to test hypotheses or address research questions such as sample characteristics, sample size, type of employees, teams, or organisation; providing recommendations for an effective data collection; providing recommendations for research access; and sampling techniques) should management researchers not use ChatGPT?

8. Data analysis:
   a) Can you please tell me what is the best way of using ChatGPT in management research for data analysis including providing recommendations for data management; providing recommendations for the data analysis; conducting the data analysis (e.g., descriptive statistics, t-tests, ANOVA regression analysis, factor analysis, structural equation modelling, and multilevel analysis); providing recommendations for how to present the data; data visualisation; and writing up results in a descriptive way based on a results table?
   b) For which tasks related to data analysis (including providing recommendations for data management; providing recommendations for the data analysis; conducting the data analysis (e.g., descriptive statistics, t-tests, ANOVA regression analysis, factor analysis, structural equation modelling, and multilevel analysis); providing recommendations for how to present the data; data visualisation; writing up results in a descriptive way based on a results table) should management researchers not use ChatGPT?

9. Discussion section of a manuscript:
   a) Can you please tell me what is the best way of using ChatGPT in management research for the discussion of an article including providing ideas for the theoretical contributions of a study, providing ideas for practical contributions of a study, providing ideas for the limitations of a study, providing ideas for the strengths of a study, providing ideas for future research recommendations, and providing ideas for a short conclusion for a study?
   b) For which tasks related to the discussion of academic articles (including providing ideas for the theoretical contributions of a study, providing ideas for the practical contributions of a study, providing ideas for the limitations of a study, providing ideas for the strengths of a study, providing ideas for future research recommendations, and providing ideas for a short conclusion for a study) should management researchers not use ChatGPT?

The Future of Human–AI Collaboration in Research

4

Redesigning Inquiry Through Symbiotic Partnerships

INTRODUCTION

The rapid evolution of AI has moved it from the periphery of research methodology to the very centre of knowledge production. As the chapters in this volume demonstrate, AI systems are no longer merely passive tools for automation; they have become active, socio-technical partners that redefine the epistemological foundations of scientific inquiry. From the deployment of humanoid robots in deep-sea exploration and hazardous disaster zones to the use of generative models as reflective partners in educational settings, AI is extending the analytical capacity of researchers and accelerating the pace of discovery across diverse fields. This shift, however, brings a dual responsibility:

DOI: 10.1201/9781003786405-5

the promise of enhanced efficiency must be balanced against the imperative of ethical accountability and human oversight.

This book has argued for a human-centred and governance-aware understanding of AI in research, spanning both embodied systems and generative models. The preceding chapters have analysed how abstract ethical principles – transparency, justice, non-maleficence, responsibility, and privacy – can be translated into research-relevant practices. Whether through the Reflective Partnership Framework for teacher-researchers or practical guidelines for management scholars, a recurring theme has emerged: ethics is not a barrier to innovation but an enabling condition for scientific legitimacy and public trust. This concluding chapter synthesises these perspectives to map the future of human–AI collaboration (HAIC), emphasising that the ultimate goal is a symbiotic relationship that preserves human agency in an increasingly automated world.

PERSPECTIVES ON HUMAN–AI COLLABORATION

The conceptualisation of AI has undergone a fundamental shift from viewing it as a static automation tool to recognising it as an active collaborative agent. While collaborative information behaviour scholarship has traditionally focused on human-to-human interaction, there is an evolving and urgent need to examine AI as a socio-technical partner (Atolagbe-Olaoye et al., 2025). This shift is characterised by the emergence of a 'missing middle' in the workforce, where AI does not replace labour but instead creates novel roles for humans as trainers, explainers, and sustainers (Daugherty & Euchner, 2020). This paradigm moves away from total automation towards augmentation, where redesigned workflows allow AI systems to adapt to human needs. Such a transition enables organisations to unlock innovation through a symbiotic relationship rather than mere task delegation, ensuring that technology serves to amplify rather than suppress human potential within professional environments.

Building on this systemic view, HAIC is increasingly defined as a dynamic, non-linear socio-technical system. Hybrid performance cannot be predicted by AI accuracy alone; instead, it emerges from the complex interplay of dozens of interdependent factors, including task risk, workflow configuration, and role clarity (Gondöcs et al., 2025). This perspective suggests that effective human–AI teaming requires the same foundations as high-performing human teams, specifically shared mental models, transparency, and meaningful human control (National Academies of Sciences, Engineering, and Medicine, 2022). To move beyond simple tool use, collaboration must be structured through specific frameworks that clarify division-of-labour configurations (Aman et al., 2025). In this context, HAIC is primarily a socio-organisational design challenge where success depends on balancing human judgement with AI precision within ethically grounded and structured feedback loops that prioritise accountability and safety.

Central to the success of these socio-technical systems is the complex mechanism of trust calibration. Organisations can foster reliable partnerships by actively configuring design-relevant elements such as benevolence, integrity, and the propensity to trust (Do Khac & Leyer, 2026). Interestingly, research suggests that trust in AI is not a uniform construct but is often asymmetric; for instance, while humans may lack affective or emotional trust in AI teammates compared to human peers, they frequently maintain high levels of cognitive trust (Georganta & Ulfert, 2024). This distinction allows for rational reliance on AI competence even when a deeper emotional connection is absent. Looking towards 2030, proponents of augmented intelligence envision AI as an adaptive team member that supports not only task performance but also team dynamics and human well-being (Fischer, 2023). The goal of design is not to maximise trust, but to ensure it is accurately aligned with the system's actual capabilities.

The physical and social design of the AI interface also plays a nuanced role in how collaboration unfolds. Contrary to popular belief, anthropomorphic or human-like design is not necessarily the primary driver of effective teamwork (Siemon et al., 2025). Experimental evidence suggests that an AI's perceived social presence influences a team's motivation indirectly by shaping how members depend on one another and their overall commitment to the team (Siemon et al., 2025). Rather than focusing on making AI look human, effective collaboration depends more on the AI being socially embedded within team processes and being understandable to its human partners. This aligns with broader frameworks that emphasise five distinct collaboration clusters, suggesting that design principles like initiative, adaptability, and explicability are more vital for sustainable systems than mere visual mimicry (Puerta-Beldarrain et al., 2025). These principles are especially critical in knowledge-intensive domains where the logic behind AI suggestions must be transparent.

In the realm of creativity and knowledge production, HAIC functions as a partnership that enhances productivity and fosters interdisciplinary synthesis. Deep learning systems are most valuable when designed as adaptive teammates that complement human creativity rather than attempting to automate it entirely (Mahmud et al., 2023). Effective symbiosis in these creative fields relies on human-in-the-loop decision-making to overcome the current limitations of shallow cognitive modelling in AI (Mahmud et al., 2023). Furthermore, AI-generated content tools have been shown to significantly improve communication and knowledge synthesis across different academic and professional fields (Yan & Qianjun, 2025). However, this collaboration must be strategically scaffolded to be effective. Without careful pedagogical and professional design, there is a significant risk that overreliance on AI could undermine critical evaluation skills and the integrity of individual disciplines, necessitating constant human oversight and ethical governance (Yan & Qianjun, 2025).

The impact of HAIC is also visible at the macro-organisational level, where it serves as a catalyst for efficiency and skill acquisition. Empirical evidence from large-scale econometric analyses shows that the coordinated development of human capital and AI significantly improves firm input-output efficiency (Sun & Song, 2025). This technological catch-up is particularly effective when AI is positioned as a partner rather than a substitution mechanism for human workers. A unique dimension of this partnership is machine mentoring, in which AI systems function as implicit mentors that transfer procedural and tacit knowledge to humans during task execution (Vicente & Cabitza, 2025). While this can accelerate skill acquisition for novices, it introduces risks of deskilling and the transmission of algorithmic bias (Vicente & Cabitza, 2025). Therefore, the organisational benefit of HAIC is highly dependent on contextual readiness, R&D investment, and the implementation of safeguards to ensure that AI enhances human learning.

The effectiveness of HAIC is fundamentally moderated by cultural and ethical contexts. Controlled experiments demonstrate that cultural background dictates how individuals prefer to interact with AI, particularly regarding decision control (Sui et al., 2025). For example, individuals from culturally tight environments show a higher willingness to collaborate only when they retain high levels of decision control to protect their human identity (Sui et al., 2025). This highlights that a one-size-fits-all approach to HAIC design is likely to fail in a globalised workforce. Managing these cultural nuances, alongside risks like hallucinations and bias in generative AI, requires a human-centred approach that prioritises AI literacy (Nah et al., 2023). By maintaining human oversight and ethical governance, organisations can ensure that AI remains an intelligence-augmenting partner rather than a liability. The future of HAIC lies in creating adaptive, transparent systems that respect human agency across diverse global and cultural contexts.

HUMAN–AI COLLABORATION IN THE RESEARCH PROCESS

The integration of AI into the research lifecycle marks a transition from viewing it as a simple processing tool to recognising it as a methodological collaborator.

This shift is predicated on the development of mutual trust, where researchers rely on AI as a stable computing infrastructure while AI systems earn social trust through ethical operations, such as transparency and privacy (Kashima et al., 2024). This reciprocal relationship allows both parties to adapt to one another, creating a partnership capable of solving complex problems that neither could address in isolation. By moving away from a 'death of research' narrative, scholars argue for a symbiotic model where AI excels at large-scale data processing and pattern recognition, while the core drivers of meaningful discovery – creativity, contextual interpretation, and ethical judgement – remain irreducibly human (Salah et al., 2023). In this view, AI is most valuable when it is embedded within human-led workflows that prioritise human agency.

To facilitate this partnership, recent architectural frameworks emphasise embedding principles of human–data interaction (HDI) directly into generative AI systems. By focusing on legibility, agency, and negotiability, these designs transform opaque algorithms into adaptive partners capable of transparent reasoning (Durango et al., 2025). Such HDI-enhanced systems support ethically grounded co-creation by allowing researchers to maintain meaningful control over the AI's internal logic. This vision is further expanded by the concept of generative artificial experts (GAEs), which represent a qualitative leap beyond general-purpose AI. These agents possess bounded autonomy and deep domain expertise, functioning as semi-autonomous collaborators embedded in knowledge work (Sowa & Przegalinska, 2025). By utilising synthetic personas and multimodal capabilities, GAEs can enhance productivity and democratise knowledge while preserving the necessary human oversight to ensure that the outputs remain aligned with rigorous disciplinary standards and ethical accountability.

In the context of evidence synthesis and literature reviews, AI is increasingly positioned as a supportive collaborator rather than an autonomous evaluator. While tools like ChatGPT can perform well in structured tasks such as title and abstract screening, they exhibit significant limitations in interpretative synthesis, including high hallucination rates (Adel & Alani, 2025). Empirical evaluations of source-grounded tools like NotebookLM suggest they are most effective as conversational partners for cross-checking and idea generation, provided that the researcher retains full responsibility for verification and interpretative judgement (Shor et al., 2025). Consequently, frameworks such as the Systematic Research Processing Framework have been proposed to embed validation checkpoints into the workflow (Adel & Alani, 2025). These models ensure that human-in-the-loop oversight remains the primary mechanism for maintaining validity, allowing AI to surface novel insights without compromising the accuracy or transparency required for scholarly rigour (Lucio et al., 2025).

The role of the human expert remains particularly critical in the technical execution of systematic searches. Comparisons between AI-generated search strategies and the search strategy employed by the authors of a systematic review published in the Cochrane Database of Systematic Reviews reveal that AI outputs are often less comprehensive and more prone to errors (Bourgeois & Ellingson, 2025). Human expertise is essential for managing controlled vocabularies and ensuring the methodological rigour and reproducibility demanded by systematic review standards. Currently, it seems that AI tools cannot replace the specialised role of librarians; instead, they serve as complementary aids for citation tracking and database selection within a librarian-centred collaboration (Park, 2025). This positioning ensures that the search process remains exhaustive and transparent. By treating AI as an assistant rather than an autonomous replacement, researchers can leverage its speed for routine tasks while relying on human experts to navigate the nuanced complexities of information retrieval and theory-building.

AI also functions as a methodological amplifier in large-scale research synthesis, helping to surface thematic blind spots that human researchers might overlook. When embedded in supervised, human-led workflows, AI tools can accelerate sensemaking and bridge the gap between academic evaluation and societal impact (Steingard & Rodenburg, 2025). This augmentative power is also evident in qualitative inquiry, where the AbductivAI model reconceptualises AI as a co-researcher (Costa et al., 2025). In this abductive workflow, AI agents act as reflexive partners in coding and pattern detection, while the human researcher retains the epistemic authority to perform final theory refinement (Costa et al., 2025). This collaboration fundamentally reshapes how qualitative knowledge is produced, ensuring that rigour and reflexivity are maintained through explicitly designed human–AI interactions that emphasise the researcher's final interpretative authority.

Beyond text-based synthesis, human-centred AI systems are being designed as adaptable partners in specialised scientific fields, such as biological research. For instance, the concept of collective curation intelligence suggests that AI-based digital curators can handle routine anomaly detection and cross-dataset linking in biodiversity collections (Stenhouse et al., 2025). This allows human curators to focus on interpretation and policy-making, transforming static data into dynamic infrastructures for global discovery. Such systems work best when they are modular and customisable, allowing users to retain agency while benefiting from large-scale automated analysis (Karimli, 2025). Whether through herbarium analysis or assistive interfaces, these multimodal models demonstrate that effective collaboration emerges when AI is treated as an extension of human capability, enabling scientists to tackle massive data challenges that were previously insurmountable.

In educational and training settings, the collaborative potential of AI must be carefully managed to ensure it enhances rather than replaces human learning. Research indicates that while AI can improve performance in scientific problem-solving, students often treat it as a simple answer-providing tool rather than a peer-like collaborator (Tong et al., 2025). This can lead to smaller learning gains compared to human-to-human collaboration, particularly when the AI provides inconsistent responses or errors. To address this, higher education must reconceptualise AI as a collaborative cognitive partner, integrating it through metacognitively informed pedagogy (Atchley et al., 2024). By teaching students to critically evaluate, regulate, and reflect on their AI use, educators can position technology as a team member that supports higher-order thinking and communication skills. This approach ensures that the human-in-the-loop philosophy starts with the development of the researchers and practitioners of the future.

Finally, the integration of generative AI as a methodological collaborator enables the expansion of experimental realism and the safe use of synthetic data. By serving as an augmentative partner, AI allows researchers to simulate complex scenarios and manage vast datasets that would be impossible to handle manually (Rossi et al., 2024). However, the benefits of such high-level collaboration are entirely contingent on the maintenance of ethical guidelines and rigorous oversight to prevent hallucinations and bias. The emerging consensus across these diverse research domains is that HAIC is not a replacement for human intellect but a redesign of the research process itself. By preserving human epistemic authority and focusing on adaptive, transparent partnerships, the research community can harness AI to accelerate discovery while remaining anchored in the ethical and interpretative values that define scientific inquiry.

CONCLUSION

As we look towards the future of research, the integration of AI signifies a fundamental redesign of the research process itself rather than a mere replacement for human intellect. The case studies and frameworks presented throughout this volume provide a roadmap for navigating this transition responsibly. To ensure that AI remains an intelligence-augmenting partner, researchers and institutions must prioritise the development of digital literacy and generative knowing, where human judgement acts as the final arbiter of truth and ethical integrity. The sustainability of this collaboration depends on our ability to maintain clear lines of accountability, even as systems achieve higher levels of autonomy.

In conclusion, the path forward for HAIC in research is paved by interdisciplinary cooperation and a steadfast commitment to human-centric design. By embedding ethical precepts throughout the research lifecycle, from initial question formulation to final dissemination, we can protect the validity of AI-mediated findings and the social benefit of scientific innovation. As humanoid robots and generative agents become standard components of our research infrastructure, the capacity to foster mutual trust and preserve human dignity will remain the most critical metrics of success. The future of discovery lies in a partnership where technology amplifies human creativity, ensuring that the pursuit of knowledge remains a profoundly human endeavour.

References

Abunaseer, H. (2023). The use of generative AI in education: Applications and impact. In R. Power (Ed.), *Technology and the curriculum: Summer 2023*. Pressbooks.

Acemoglu, D., & Restrepo, P. (2020). Robots and jobs: Evidence from US labor markets. *Journal of Political Economy*, *128*(6), 2188–2244. https://doi.org/10.1086/705716

Ackerman, E. (2016, April 28). Stanford's humanoid diving robot takes on undersea archaeology and coral reefs. *IEEE Spectrum*. https://spectrum.ieee.org/stanford-ocean-one-humanoid-diving-robot

Adamovic, M. (2020). Analyzing discrimination in recruitment: A guide and best practices for resume studies. *International Journal of Selection and Assessment*, *28*(4), 445–464. https://doi.org/10.1111/ijsa.12298

Adel, A., & Alani, N. (2025). Can generative AI reliably synthesise literature? Exploring hallucination issues in ChatGPT. *AI & Society*, *40*, 6799–6812. https://doi.org/10.1007/s00146-025-02406-7

Aguinis, H., & Bradley, K. J. (2014). Best practice recommendations for designing and implementing experimental vignette methodology studies. *Organizational research methods*, *17*(4), 351–371. https://doi.org/10.1177/1094428114547952

Al-Qura'n, M. (2004). Preservice teacher training through action research: The case of a preservice science teacher in change. *Mediterranean Journal of Educational Studies*, *9*(1), 21–39.

Aman, F., Abdul Hamid, S. R., Mat Isa, A., & Mohamad, M. H. S. (2025). A systematic review of trends in human–AI collaboration research. *The International Journal of Technology, Knowledge, and Society*, *21*(1), 189–217. https://doi.org/10.18848/1832-3669/CGP/v21i01/189-217

Apelgren, B.-M., Burnard, P., & Cabaroglu, N. (2015). Theory-use in teacher research. In P. Burnard, B.-M. Apelgren, & N. Cabaroglu (Eds.), *Transformative teacher research: Theory and practice for the C21st* (pp. 3–12). Sense Publishers. https://doi.org/10.1007/978-94-6209-974-6_1

Arefian, M. H., Çomoğlu, I., & Dikilitaş, K. (2024). Understanding EFL teachers' experiences of ChatGPT-driven collaborative reflective practice through a community of practice lens. *Innovation in Language Learning and Teaching*. https://doi.org/10.1080/17501229.2024.2412769

Atchley, P., Pannell, H., Wofford, K., Hopkins, M., & Atchley, R. A. (2024). Human and AI collaboration in the higher education environment: Opportunities and concerns. *Cognitive Research: Principles and Implications*, *9*, 20. https://doi.org/10.1186/s41235-024-00547-9

Atolagbe-Olaoye, A., Chang, H.-C., & Hawamdeh, S. (2025). Exploring collaborative tools in collaborative information behaviour research: A scoping review. *Journal of Information Science*. https://doi.org/10.1177/01655515251353169

Attard, K. (2020). Understanding the reflective process through self-study: A teacher educator's journey towards continuous professional development. In A. Swennen & E. White (Eds.), *Being a teacher educator* (pp. 27–42). Routledge.

Bandura, A. (1997). *Self-efficacy: The exercise of control*. W. H. Freeman.

Bass, L., Anderson-Patton, V., & Allender, J. (2002). Self-study as a way of teaching and learning: A research collaborative re-analysis of self-study teaching portfolios. In J. Loughran & T. Russell (Eds.), *Improving teacher education practice through self-study* (pp. 72–87). Routledge. https://doi.org/10.4324/9780203018637-7

Bell, E., Harley, B., & Bryman, A. (2022). *Business research methods* (6th ed.). Oxford University Press.

Bourgeois, J. P., & Ellingson, H. (2025). Ability of ChatGPT to generate systematic review search strategies compared to a published search strategy. *Medical Reference Services Quarterly*, *44*(3), 279–291. https://doi.org/10.1080/02763869.2025.2537075

Brewis, J. (2014). The ethics of researching friends: On convenience sampling in qualitative management and organization studies. *British Journal of Management*, *25*(4), 849–862. https://doi.org/10.1111/1467-8551.12064

Brookfield, S. D. (2017). *Becoming a critically reflective teacher* (2nd ed.). Jossey-Bass.

Buolamwini, J., & Gebru, T. (2018). Gender shades: Intersectional accuracy disparities in commercial gender classification. Proceedings of the 1st Conference on Fairness, Accountability and Transparency. In *Proceedings of Machine Learning Research* (pp. 77–91). http://proceedings.mlr.press/v81/buolamwini18a.html

Buontempo, F. (2025, August 17). 'Pregnancy robots' could give birth to human children in revolutionary breakthrough – and a game-changer for infertile couples. *New York Post*. https://nypost.com/2025/08/17/tech/pregnancy-robots-could-give-birth-to-human-children/

Busuttil, L. (2024). Enhancing reflective practices in pre-service educators: A case study on the role of GenAI in assessment as learning. In *HELMeTO 2024: Higher education learning methodologies and technologies online: Book of abstracts* (pp. 30–32). Editore Studium.

Cabaroglu, N. (2015). Promoting teachers as reflective practitioners. In P. Burnard, B.-M. Apelgren, & N. Cabaroglu (Eds.), *Transformative teacher research: Theory and practice for the C21st* (pp. 113–125). Sense Publishers. https://doi.org/10.1163/9789463002233_010

Cai, H., Lu, L., Han, B., Wong, L.-H., & Gu, X. (2025). Exploring pre-service teachers' reflection mediated by an AI-powered teacher dashboard in video-based professional learning: A pilot study. *Educational Technology Research and Development*, *73*(3), 1129–1154. https://doi.org/10.1007/s11423-024-10442-1

Calo, R. (2015). Robotics and the lessons of cyberlaw. *California Law Review*, *103*(3), 513–563. http://doi.org/10.2139/ssrn.2402972

Chetcuti, D. (2002). Becoming a reflective practitioner. In C. Bezzina, A. Camilleri Grima, D. Purchase & R. Sultana (Eds.), *Inside secondary schools: A Maltese reader* (pp. 155–168). Indigo Books.

China Unicom Research Institute and China Branch of BRICS Institute of Future Networks. (2025). *Applications and development prospects of humanoid robots*. https://www.wicinternet.org/pdf/ApplicationsandDevelopmentProspectsofHumanoidRobots.pdf

Chui, M., Roberts, R., & Yee, L. (2022, December 20). *Generative AI is here: How tools like ChatGPT could change your business*. McKinsey & Company. https://www.mckinsey.com/capabilities/quantumblack/our-insights/generative-ai-is-here-how-tools-like-chatgpt-could-change-your-business#/

Clancy, A., & Vince, R. (2019). Theory as fantasy: Emotional dimensions to grounded theory. *British Journal of Management*, *30*(1), 203–216. https://doi.org/10.1111/1467-8551.12304

Cochran-Smith, M., & Lytle, S. L. (2009). *Inquiry as stance: Practitioner research for the next generation*. Teachers College Press.

Coeckelbergh, M. (2023). Narrative responsibility and artificial intelligence. *AI & Society*, *38*, 2437–2450. https://doi.org/10.1007/s00146-021-01375-x

Cohen, T. (2019). How to leverage artificial intelligence to meet your diversity goals. *Strategic HR Review*, *18*(2), 62–65. https://doi.org/10.1108/SHR-12-2018-0105

Cornish, L. (2024). Reflective practice and professional development. In L. Cornish (Ed.), *(Re)learning as reflective practitioners* (pp. 109–126). Springer. https://doi.org/10.1007/978-3-031-60211-5_8

Costa, A. P., Bryda, G., Christou, P. A., & Kasperiuniene, J. (2025). AI as a co-researcher in the qualitative research workflow: Transforming human–AI collaboration. *International Journal of Qualitative Methods*, *24*. https://doi.org/10.1177/16094069251383739

Cruz, E. M. G. N. V., Valente, A., & Onori, M. (2024). Robotics applications in the hospital domain: A literature review. *Applied System Innovation*, *7*(6), 125. https://doi.org/10.3390/asi7060125

Cummings, M. L. (2017). *Artificial intelligence and the future of warfare*. Chatham House. https://www.chathamhouse.org/sites/default/files/publications/research/2017-01-26-artificial-intelligence-future-warfare-cummings-final.pdf

Dana, N. F., & Yendol-Hoppey, D. (2010). The role of inquiry-oriented learning communities and protocols in sustaining and enhancing teacher reflectivity throughout the professional lifetime. In E. G. Pultorak (Ed.), *The purposes, practices, and professionalism of teacher reflectivity: Insights for twenty-first-century teachers and students* (pp. 226–245). Bloomsbury.

Darvish, K., Penco, L., Ramos, J., Cisneros, R., Pratt, J., Yoshida, E., Ivaldi, S., & Pucci, D. (2023). Teleoperation of humanoid robots: A survey. *IEEE Transactions on Robotics*, *39*(3), 1706–1727. https://doi.org/10.1109/TRO.2023.3236952

Daugherty, P., & Euchner, J. (2020). Human + machine: Collaboration in the age of AI. *Research-Technology Management*, *63*(2), 12–17. https://doi.org/10.1080/08956308.2020.1707001

De Mauro, A., Sestino, A., & Bacconi, A. (2022). Machine learning and artificial intelligence use in marketing: A general taxonomy. *Italian Journal of Marketing*, *2022*, 439–457. https://doi.org/10.1007/s43039-022-00057-w

Defense Science Board. (2016). *Summer study on autonomy: Final report*. Office of the Under Secretary of Defense for Acquisition, Technology and Logistics. https://irp.fas.org/agency/dod/dsb/autonomy-ss.pdf

Deng, Q., Fu, C., Ban, M., & Iio, T. (2024). A systematic review on robot-assisted language learning for adults. *Frontiers in Psychology*, *15*, 1471370. https://doi.org/10.3389/fpsyg.2024.1471370

Destephe, M., Henning, A., Zecca, M., Hashimoto, K., & Takanishi, A. (2013). Perception of emotion and emotional intensity in humanoid robots gait. In *Proceedings of the IEEE International Conference on Robotics and Biomimetics* (pp. 1276–1281). IEEE. https://doi.org/10.1109/ROBIO.2013.6739640

Devlin, K. (2018). *Turned on: Science, sex and robots*. Bloomsbury Sigma.

Dewey, J. (1933). *How we think*. University of Wisconsin Press.

Di Nuovo, A. G., Marocco, D., Di Nuovo, S., & Cangelosi, A. (2013). Autonomous learning in humanoid robotics through mental imagery. *Neural Networks*, *41*, 147–155. https://doi.org/10.1016/j.neunet.2012.09.019

Diftler, M. A., Mehling, J. S., Abdallah, M. E., Radford, N. A., Bridgwater, L. B., Sanders, A. M., Askew, R. S., Linn, D. M., Yamokoski, J. D., Permenter, F. A., Hargrave, B. K., Platt, R., Savely, R. T., & Ambrose, R. O. (2011). Robonaut 2 – The first humanoid robot in space. In *Proceedings of the 2011 IEEE International Conference on Robotics and Automation* (pp. 2178–2183). IEEE. https://doi.org/10.1109/ICRA.2011.5979830

van Dis, E. A. M., Bollen, J., van Rooij, R., Zuidema, W., & Bockting, C. L. (2023). ChatGPT: Five priorities for research. *Nature*, *614*, 224–226. https://doi.org/10.1038/d41586-023-00288-7

Do Khac, L. T., & Leyer, M. (2026). Towards an integrative model of organizational human–AI collaboration: A semi-systematic review of the current state of the art. *Technology in Society*, *84*, 103064. https://doi.org/10.1016/j.techsoc.2025.103064

Dodd, D. (2023, February 20). ChatGPT hype sparks hopes and fears around AI. *Financial Times*. https://www.ft.com/content/ecda8734-4e3e-4e7e-9c26-ed5cbfde71e5

Duffy, B. R. (2003). Anthropomorphism and the social robot. *Robotics and Autonomous Systems*, *42*(3–4), 177–190. https://doi.org/10.1016/S0921-8890(02)00374-3

Dunn, W., Gutiérrez, X., & Ranta, L. (2023). Teacher leadership as the missing link between TBLT research and pedagogical practice. In H. Reinders (Ed.), *Language teacher leadership: New language learning and teaching environments* (pp. 229–254). Springer. https://doi.org/10.1007/978-3-031-42871-5_10

Dunwoodie, K., Macaulay, L., & Newman, A. (2023). Qualitative interviewing in the field of work and organisational psychology: Benefits, challenges and guidelines for researchers and reviewers. *Applied Psychology*, *72*(2), 863–889. https://doi.org/10.1111/apps.12414

Durango, I., Gallud, J. A., & Penichet, V. M. R. (2025). The data dance: Choreographing seamless partnerships between humans, data, and GenAI. *International Journal of Data Science and Analytics*, *20*, 3613–3640. https://doi.org/10.1007/s41060-024-00684-w

Dwivedi, Y. K., Kshetri, N., Hughes, L., Slade, E. L., Jeyaraj, A., Kar, A. K., Baabdullah, A. M., Koohang, A., Raghavan, V., Ahuja, M., Albanna, H., Albashrawi, M. A., Al-Busaidi, A. S., Balakrishnan, J., Barlette, Y., Basu, S., Bose, I., Brooks, L., Buhalis, D., … Wright, R. (2023). So what if ChatGPT wrote it? Multidisciplinary perspectives on opportunities, challenges and implications of generative conversational AI for research, practice and policy. *International*

Journal of Information Management, *71*, 102642. https://doi.org/10.1016/j.ijinfomgt.2023.102642

ElSayary, A. (2024). Integrating generative AI in active learning environments: Enhancing metacognition and technological skills. *Journal of Systemics, Cybernetics and Informatics*, *22*(3), 34–37. https://doi.org/10.54808/JSCI.22.03.34

Estaiteyeh, M., & McQuirter, R. (2024). Generative or degenerative?! Implications of AI tools in pre-service teacher education and reflections on instructors' professional development. *Brock Education Journal*, *33*(3), 75–98. https://doi.org/10.26522/brocked.v33i3.1176

European Commission. (2019, April 8). *Ethics guidelines for trustworthy AI*. https://digital-strategy.ec.europa.eu/en/library/ethics-guidelines-trustworthy-ai

European Commission. (2025). *A European Strategy for Artificial Intelligence in Science Paving the way for the Resource for AI Science in Europe (RAISE)*. https://eur-lex.europa.eu/legal-content/EN/TXT/PDF/?uri=CELEX:52025DC0724

European Parliament & Council of the European Union. (2016). *Regulation (EU) 2016/679 of the European Parliament and of the Council of 27 April 2016 on the protection of natural persons with regard to the processing of personal data and on the free movement of such data (General Data Protection Regulation). Official Journal of the European Union, L 119*, 1–88. https://eur-lex.europa.eu/eli/reg/2016/679/oj

European Union. (2024). Regulation (EU) 2024/1689 of the European Parliament and of the Council of 13 June 2024 laying down harmonised rules on artificial intelligence (Artificial Intelligence Act) and amending Regulations (EC) No 300/2008, (EU) No 167/2013, (EU) No 168/2013, (EU) 2018/858, (EU) 2018/1139 and (EU) 2019/2144 and Directives 2014/90/EU, (EU) 2016/797 and (EU) 2020/1828. Official Journal of the European Union, L 2024/1689. https://data.europa.eu/eli/reg/2024/1689/oj

Farrell, T. S. C. (2016). Anniversary article: The practices of encouraging TESOL teachers to engage in reflective practice: An appraisal of recent research contributions. *Language Teaching Research*, *20*(2), 223–247. https://doi.org/10.1177/1362168815617335

Farrell, T. S. C. (2020). *Reflective teaching*. TESOL International Association.

Farrell, T. S. C. (2023). 'Teacher you are stupid!' Cultivating and nurturing a reflective disposition in leaders. In H. Reinders (Ed.), *Language teacher leadership: New language learning and teaching environments* (pp. 19–38). Springer. https://doi.org/10.1007/978-3-031-42871-5_2

Fathian, Z., & Farahian, M. (2021). Online collaborative action research in an EFL context: The effect on teachers' reflective practice. *Information Technologies and Learning Tools*, *84*(4), 158–175. https://doi.org/10.33407/itlt.v84i4.4541

Fessl, A., Divitini, M., & Maitz, K. (2023). Transferring digital competences for teaching from theory into practice through reflection. In O. Viberg, I. Jivet, P. Muñoz-Merino, M. Perifanou, & T. Papathoma (Eds.), *Responsive and sustainable educational futures: EC-TEL 2023* (pp. 554–559). Springer. https://doi.org/10.1007/978-3-031-42682-7_41

Fischer, F. (2023). Future collaboration between humans and AI: "I strive to make you feel good," says my AI colleague in 2030. In I. Knappertsbusch & K. Gondlach

(Eds.), *Work and AI 2030: Challenges and strategies for tomorrow's work* (pp. 21–28). Springer. https://doi.org/10.1007/978-3-658-40232-7_3

Fisher, S. L., Bonaccio, S., Jetha, A., Winkler, M., Birch, G. E., & Gignac, M. A. M. (2023). Guidelines for conducting partnered research in applied psychology: An illustration from disability research in employment contexts. *Applied Psychology*, *72*(4), 1367–1391. https://doi.org/10.1111/apps.12438

Floridi, L. (2019). Translating principles into practices of digital ethics: Five risks of being unethical. *Philosophy & Technology*, *32*, 185–193. https://doi.org/10.1007/s13347-019-00354-x

Floridi, L., & Cowls, J. (2019). A unified framework of five principles for AI in society. *Harvard Data Science Review*, *1*(1). https://doi.org/10.1162/99608f92.8cd550d1

Georganta, E., & Ulfert, A.-S. (2024). My colleague is an AI! Trust differences between AI and human teammates. *Team Performance Management: An International Journal*, *30*(1–2), 23–37. https://doi.org/10.1108/TPM-07-2023-0053

Ghiasvand, F., & Seyri, H. (2025). A collaborative reflection on the synergy of artificial intelligence (AI) and language teacher identity reconstruction. *Teaching and Teacher Education*, *160*, 105022. https://doi.org/10.1016/j.tate.2025.105022

Gondöcs, D., Horváth, S., & Dörfler, V. (2025). Uncovering the dynamics of human–AI hybrid performance: A qualitative meta-analysis of empirical studies. *International Journal of Human–Computer Studies*, *205*, 103622. https://doi.org/10.1016/j.ijhcs.2025.103622

Hagevik, R., Aydeniz, M., & Rowell, C. G. (2012). Using action research in middle level teacher education to evaluate and deepen reflective practice. *Teaching and Teacher Education*, *28*(5), 675–684. https://doi.org/10.1016/j.tate.2012.02.006

Hanks, J. (2021). Co-production and multimodality: Learners as co-researchers exploring practice. *Educational Action Research*, *29*(3), 462–482. https://doi.org/10.1080/09650792.2020.1812417

Hartmann, U., Kindlinger, M., & Trempler, K. (2021). Integrating information from multiple texts relates to pre-service teachers' epistemic products for reflective teaching practice. *Teaching and Teacher Education*, *97*, 103205. https://doi.org/10.1016/j.tate.2020.103205

Hazlehurst, C., Etter, M., & Brouthers, K. D. (2023). Towards a unified typology of digital communication technologies in international business: a tool for management and research. *Multinational Business Review*, *31*(4), 437–458. https://doi.org/10.1108/MBR-01-2023-0011

Hickok, M. (2021). Lessons learned from AI ethics principles for future actions. *AI and Ethics*, *1*, 41–47. https://doi.org/10.1007/s43681-020-00008-1

Houser, K. A. (2019). Can AI solve the diversity problem in the tech industry? Mitigating noise and bias in employment decision-making. *Stanford Technology Law Review*, *22*, 290–354.

Hu, Y. (2025). Generative AI, communication, and stereotypes: Learning critical AI literacy through experience, analysis, and reflection. *Communication Teacher*, *39*(1), 6–12. https://doi.org/10.1080/17404622.2024.2397065

Human Rights Watch. (2012, November 19). *Losing humanity: The case against killer robots*. https://www.hrw.org/report/2012/11/19/losing-humanity/case-against-killer-robots

Hutson, J. (2025). *The rise of AI in academic inquiry*. IGI Global.
ISO. (2014). *ISO 13482:2014 Robots and robotic devices – Safety requirements for personal care robots*. International Organization for Standardization. https://www.iso.org/standard/53820.html
ISO/IEC. (2023). *ISO/IEC 23894:2023 Information technology – Artificial intelligence – Guidance on risk management*. International Organization for Standardization/International Electrotechnical Commission. https://www.iso.org/standard/77304.html
ISO/TS. (2016). *ISO/TS 15066:2016 Robots and robotic devices – Collaborative robots*. International Organization for Standardization/Technical Committee. https://www.iso.org/standard/62996.html
Jafari, M., Saeedvand, S., & Aghdasi, H. S. (2019). A hybrid Q-learning algorithm to score a moving ball for humanoid robots. In *Proceedings of the 5th Conference on Knowledge-Based Engineering and Innovation (KBEI)* (pp. 498–503). IEEE. https://doi.org/10.1109/KBEI.2019.8735027
James, D. (2023, February 17). What does ChatGPT mean for the future of business? *Entrepreneur*. https://www.entrepreneur.com/science-technology/what-does-chatgpt-mean-for-the-future-of-business/445020
Jeffers, J. R., Auyang, A. G., & Grabowski, A. M. (2015). The correlation between metabolic and individual leg mechanical power during walking at different slopes and velocities. *Journal of Biomechanics*, *48*(11), 2919–2924. https://doi.org/10.1016/j.jbiomech.2015.04.023
Jobin, A., Ienca, M., & Vayena, E. (2019). The global landscape of AI ethics guidelines. *Nature Machine Intelligence*, *1*, 389–399. https://doi.org/10.1038/s42256-019-0088-2
Jochum, E., Millar, P., & Nuñez, D. (2017). Sequence and chance: Design and control methods for entertainment robots. *Robotics and Autonomous Systems*, *87*, 372–380. https://doi.org/10.1016/j.robot.2016.08.019
Johannessen, W. H. (2024). Modelling teachers' reflective practice. *Reflective Practice*, *25*(6), 784–798. https://doi.org/10.1080/14623943.2024.2406934
Jones, M. (2024). Embedding reflection in professional practice. In L. Cornish (Ed.), *(Re)learning as reflective practitioners* (pp. 87–107). Springer. https://doi.org/10.1007/978-3-031-60211-5_7
Jou, M., Kuo, T.-H., Chiang, Y.-C., Hao, Y., & Huang, C.-C. (2025). Integrating generative AI in teacher education: A qualitative exploration of TPACK growth and critical reflection. *The Turkish Online Journal of Educational Technology*, *24*(3), 54–66.
Karimli, F. (2025). *Advancing human–AI collaboration: Multimodal systems for accessibility, research, and learning* [Master's thesis, Boston University]. https://hdl.handle.net/2144/49681
Kashima, H., Oyama, S., Arai, H., & Mori, J. (2024). Trustworthy human computation: A survey. *Artificial Intelligence Review*, *57*, 322. https://doi.org/10.1007/s10462-024-10974-1
Kasneci, E., Sessler, K., Küchemann, S., Bannert, M., Dementieva, D., Fischer, F., Gasser, U., Groh, G., Günnemann, S., Hüllermeier, E., Krusche, S., Kutyniok, G., Michaeli, T., Nerdel, C., Pfeffer, J., Poquet, O., Sailer, M., Schmidt, A.,

Seidel, T., Stadler, M., Weller, J., Kuhn, J., & Kasneci, G. (2023). ChatGPT for good? On opportunities and challenges of large language models for education. *Learning and Individual Differences*, *103*, 102274. https://doi.org/10.1016/j.lindif.2023.102274

Keith, R., & La, H. M. (2024). *Review of autonomous mobile robots for the warehouse environment* (arXiv:2406.08333v1). arXiv. https://doi.org/10.48550/arXiv.2406.08333

Kober, J., Glisson, M., & Mistry, M. (2012). Playing catch and juggling with a humanoid robot. In *Proceedings of the 12th IEEE-RAS International Conference on Humanoid Robots (Humanoids 2012)* (pp. 875–881). IEEE. https://doi.org/10.1109/HUMANOIDS.2012.6651623

Kung, T. H., Cheatham, M., Medenilla, A., Sillos, C., De Leon, L., Elepaño, C., Madriaga, M., Aggabao, R., Diaz-Candido, G., Maningo, J., & Tseng, V. (2023). Performance of ChatGPT on USMLE: Potential for AI-assisted medical education using large language models. *PLOS Digital Health*, *2*(2), e0000198. https://doi.org/10.1371/journal.pdig.0000198

Lackner, T., Hermann, J., Kuhn, C., & Palm, D. (2024). Review of autonomous mobile robots in intralogistics: State-of-the-art, limitations and research gaps. *Procedia CIRP*, *130*, 930–935. https://doi.org/10.1016/j.procir.2024.10.187

Lanese, N. (2025, August 23). 'Pregnancy robot from China' is fake, but is the technology behind it possible? *LiveScience*. https://www.livescience.com/health/fertility-pregnancy-birth/pregnancy-robot-from-china-is-fake-but-is-the-technology-behind-it-possible

Lee, S. C. (2018). Pre-service teachers' progressive reflective practices using weekly journals in an action research project. *The Journal of Asia TEFL*, *15*(1), 242–249. https://doi.org/10.18823/asiatefl.2018.15.1.19.242

Lee, U., Jeong, Y., Koh, J., Byun, G., Lee, Y., Lee, H., Eun, S., Moon, J., Lim, C., & Kim, H. (2024). I see you: Teacher analytics with GPT-4 vision-powered observational assessment. *Smart Learning Environments*, *11*, 48. https://doi.org/10.1186/s40561-024-00335-4

Lee, S. H., Kim, J. S., & Yu, S. (2025). The impact of care robots on older adults: A systematic review. *Geriatric Nursing*, *65*, 103507. https://doi.org/10.1016/j.gerinurse.2025.103507

Lewis, M., Sycara, K., & Walker, P. (2018). The role of trust in human-robot interaction. In H. A. Abbass, J. Scholz, & D. Reid (Eds.), *Foundations of trusted autonomy* (pp. 135–159). Springer. https://doi.org/10.1007/978-3-319-64816-3_8

Lim, A., & Nicolaides, A. (2024). Becoming-with-AI: Rethinking professional knowledge through generative knowing. *Reflective Practice*, *25*(3), 391–405. https://doi.org/10.1080/14623943.2024.2321227

Liu, Q., Chou, J., & Feng, H. (2025). Effect of teachers' self-efficacy with generative AI and reflection on students' second language achievement. *Computer Assisted Language Learning*. https://doi.org/10.1080/09588221.2025.2498095

Lucio, R., Harris, A., Creswell Báez, J., Campbell, M., & Ricciardelli, L. A. (2025). Artificial intelligence in systematic literature reviews: Social work ethics, application, and feasibility. *Journal of Evidence-Based Social Work*. https://doi.org/10.1080/26408066.2025.2548853

Lukáčová, Z. (2020). On the nature of reflective practice in English language teaching: Importance, successful realization and challenges. *Malta Review of Educational Research, 14*(1), 115–128.

Mahmud, B., Hong, G., & Fong, B. (2023). A study of human–AI symbiosis for creative work: Recent developments and future directions in deep learning. *ACM Transactions on Multimedia Computing, Communications and Applications, 20*(2), 47. https://doi.org/10.1145/3542698

Malayil, J. (2025, September 26). Chinese tech firm is allegedly working on the world's first "gestation robot". *Interesting Engineering.* https://interestingengineering.com/innovation/china-worlds-first-pregnancy-humanoid-robot

Marshall, T., Keville, S., Cain, A., & Adler, J. R. (2021). On being open-minded, wholehearted, and responsible: A review and synthesis exploring factors enabling practitioner development in reflective practice. *Reflective Practice, 22*(6), 860–876. https://doi.org/10.1080/14623943.2021.1976131

Marshall, T., Keville, S., Cain, A., & Adler, J. R. (2022). Facilitating reflection: A review and synthesis of the factors enabling effective facilitation of reflective practice. *Reflective Practice, 23*(4), 483–496. https://doi.org/10.1080/14623943.2022.2064444

Maxwell, T. W. (2024). Using action research and structured feedback to develop reflection. In L. Cornish (Ed.), *(Re)learning as reflective practitioners* (pp. 71–83). Springer. https://doi.org/10.1007/978-3-031-60211-5_6

Meng, X.-P., Guo, X.-G., Fang, J.-W., Chen, J., & Huang, L.-F. (2025). Fostering pre-service teachers' generative AI literacy and critical thinking: An RSCQA approach. *Educational Technology & Society, 28*(3), 202–225. https://doi.org/10.30191/ETS.202507_28(3).TP01

Miller, I. K., Cunha, M. I. A., & Allwright, D. (2021). Teachers as practitioners of learning: The lens of exploratory practice. *Educational Action Research, 29*(3), 447–461. https://doi.org/10.1080/09650792.2020.1842780

Mirowska, A., & Mesnet, L. (2022). Preferring the devil you know: Potential applicant reactions to artificial intelligence evaluation of interviews. *Human Resource Management Journal, 32*(2), 364–383. https://doi.org/10.1111/1748-8583.12393

Mittelstadt, B. D., Allo, P., Taddeo, M., Wachter, S., & Floridi, L. (2016). The ethics of algorithms: Mapping the debate. *Big Data & Society, 3*(2), 1–21. https://doi.org/10.1177/2053951716679679

Munby, H., & Russell, T. (1994). The authority of experience in learning to teach: Messages from a physics methods class. *Journal of Teacher Education, 45*, 86–95. https://doi.org/10.1177/0022487194045002002

Murphy, R. R. (2014). *Disaster robotics.* MIT Press.

Murphy, R., Gandudi, V. B. M., Adams, J., Clendenin, A., & Moats, J. (2021). Adoption of robots for disasters: Lessons from the response to COVID-19. *Foundations and Trends in Robotics, 9*(2), 130–200. https://doi.org/10.1561/2300000062

Nah, F. F.-H., Zheng, R., Cai, J., Siau, K., & Chen, L. (2023). Generative AI and ChatGPT: Applications, challenges, and AI–human collaboration. *Journal of Information Technology Case and Application Research, 25*(3), 277–304. https://doi.org/10.1080/15228053.2023.2233814

NASA. (2023). *Valkyrie: NASA's first bipedal humanoid robot* (Fact sheet). NASA Johnson Space Center. https://www.nasa.gov/wp-content/uploads/2023/06/r5-fact-sheet.pdf

National Academies of Sciences, Engineering, and Medicine. (2022). *Human–AI teaming: State-of-the-art and research needs.* The National Academies Press. https://doi.org/10.17226/26355

National Commission for the Protection of Human Subjects of Biomedical and Behavioral Research. (1979). *The Belmont report: Ethical principles and guidelines for the protection of human subjects of research.* U.S. Government Printing Office. https://www.hhs.gov/ohrp/sites/default/files/the-belmont-report-508c_FINAL.pdf

Newton, D. P., & Newton, L. D. (2019). Humanoid robots as teachers and a proposed code of practice. *Frontiers in Education*, *4*, 125. https://doi.org/10.3389/feduc.2019.00125

Nguyen, H., & Nguyen, A. (2025). Reflective practices and self-regulated learning in designing with generative artificial intelligence: An ordered network analysis. *Journal of Science Education and Technology*, *34*, 1178–1192 https://doi.org/10.1007/s10956-024-10175-z

Nolan, B. (2023, January 30). Here are the schools and colleges that have banned the use of ChatGPT over plagiarism and misinformation fears. *Business Insider.* https://www.businessinsider.com/chatgpt-schools-colleges-ban-plagiarism-misinformation-education-2023-1

Oates, C., & Mynott, J. P. (2025). More-than-human centred reflection: Addressing the fiction of reflective practice in teacher education. *Research in Education*, 1–20. https://doi.org/10.1177/00345237251317373

OpenAI. (2022, November 30). *Introducing ChatGPT.* https://openai.com/blog/chatgpt

Ortega-Bolaños, R., Bernal-Salcedo, J., Germán Ortiz, M., Galeano Sarmiento, J., Ruz, G. A., & Tabares-Soto, R. (2024). Applying the ethics of AI: A systematic review of tools for developing and assessing AI-based systems. *Artificial Intelligence Review*, *57*, 110. https://doi.org/10.1007/s10462-024-10740-3

Osmanović Zajić, J., & Maksimović, J. (2020). Contemporary teachers' action research – basis for the development of reflective practice in education. *Research in Pedagogy*, *10*(2), 354–366. https://doi.org/10.5937/IstrPed2002354O

Outamgharte, B., Yeou, M., & Zyad, H. (2025). Teacher–AI collaboration for reflective practice: Exploring perceptions, practices, and impact among Moroccan EFL teachers. *Reflective Practice*, *26*(5), 645–659. https://doi.org/10.1080/14623943.2025.2494319

Paris, M. (2023, February 3). ChatGPT hits 100 million users, Google invests in AI Bot and CatGPT goes viral. *Forbes.* https://www.forbes.com/sites/martineparis/2023/02/03/chatgpt-hits-100-million-microsoft-unleashes-ai-bots-and-catgpt-goes-viral/

Park, S. G. (2025). AI and systematic reviews: Can AI tools replace librarians in the systematic search process? *Science & Technology Libraries.* https://doi.org/10.1080/0194262X.2025.2521519

Parkison, P. T. (2009). Field-based preservice teacher research: Facilitating reflective professional practice. *Teaching and Teacher Education*, *25*(5), 798–804. https://doi.org/10.1016/j.tate.2008.11.017

Phan, N. T. V., & Trinh, Q. L. (2025). Reflection from teachers as graduates: How has generative AI affected personal agency in academic writing? *Reflective Practice.* https://doi.org/10.1080/14623943.2025.2533839

Phillips, T. (2024). *Investigating design affordances of artificial intelligence for teacher reflection* [Doctoral dissertation, Indiana University].

Phillips, T. M., Saleh, A., & Ozogul, G. (2023). An AI toolkit to support teacher reflection. *International Journal of Artificial Intelligence in Education, 33*(3), 635–658. https://doi.org/10.1007/s40593-022-00295-1

Puerta-Beldarrain, M., Gómez-Carmona, O., Sánchez-Corcuera, R., Casado-Mansilla, D., López-de-Ipiña, D., & Chen, L. (2025). A multifaceted vision of the human–AI collaboration: A comprehensive review. *IEEE Access, 13*, 29375–29405. https://doi.org/10.1109/ACCESS.2025.3536095

Qing-Li, H., Torres, M. N., & Shi-Ji, F. (2019). Collaborative action research for preparing teachers as reflective practitioners. *Systemic Practice and Action Research, 32*(4), 411–427. https://doi.org/10.1007/s11213-018-9461-z

Ragno, L., Borboni, A., Vannetti, F., Amici, C., & Cusano, N. (2023). Application of social robots in healthcare: Review on characteristics, requirements, technical solutions. *Sensors, 23*(15), 6820. https://doi.org/10.3390/s23156820

Richardson, K. (2016). Sex robot matters: Slavery, the prostituted, and the rights of machines. *IEEE Technology and Society Magazine, 35*(2), 46–53. https://doi.org/10.1109/MTS.2016.2554421

Rossi, S., Rossi, M., Mukkamala, R. R., Thatcher, J. B., & Dwivedi, Y. K. (2024). Augmenting research methods with foundation models and generative AI. *International Journal of Information Management, 77*, 102749. https://doi.org/10.1016/j.ijinfomgt.2023.102749

Russell, T., & Martin, A. K. (2017). Reflective practice: Epistemological perspectives on learning from experience in teacher education. In R. Brandenburg, S. McDonough, J. Burke, & S. White (Eds.), *Reflective theory and practice in teacher education* (pp. 27–47). Springer. https://doi.org/10.1007/978-981-10-3431-2_2

Russell, T., & Martin, A. K. (2019). Making the ethical reflective turn in self-study of teacher education practice research. In R. Brandenburg & S. McDonough (Eds.), *Ethics, self-study research methodology and teacher education* (pp. 131–149). Springer. https://doi.org/10.1007/978-981-32-9135-5_9

Sadiku, M. N. O., Adekunte, P. A., & Sadiku, J. O. (2024). Robotics in the military. *International Journal of Trend in Scientific Research and Development (IJTSRD), 8*(5), 170–179. https://www.ijtsrd.com/papers/ijtsrd69345.pdf

Sahling, J., & De Carvalho, R. (2021). Understanding teacher identity as an international teacher: An autoethnographic approach to (developing) reflective practice. *Journal of Research in International Education, 20*(1), 33–49. https://doi.org/10.1177/14752409211005380

Salah, M., Abdelfattah, F., Al Halbusi, H., & Mohammed, M. (2023). Beyond the "death of research": Reimagining the human–AI collaboration in scientific research. *Changing Societies & Personalities, 7*(4), 31–46.

Sarker, S., Jamal, L., Ahmed, S. F., & Irtisam, N. (2021). Robotics and artificial intelligence in healthcare during COVID-19 pandemic: A systematic review. *Robotics and Autonomous Systems, 146*, 103902. https://doi.org/10.1016/j.robot.2021.103902

Saunders, M. N. K., Lewis, P., & Thornhill, A. (2019). *Research methods for business students* (8th ed.). Pearson.

Sawik, B., Tobis, S., Baum, E., Suwalska, A., Kropińska, S., Stachnik, K., Pérez-Bernabeu, E., Cildoz, M., Agustin, A., & Wieczorowska-Tobis, K. (2023). Robots for elderly care: Review, multi-criteria optimization model and qualitative case study. *Healthcare*, *11*(9), 1286. https://doi.org/10.3390/healthcare11091286

Schäfer, L. (2025). Reflective dialogues in negotiating the research–practice nexus: A case study of an English as a Foreign Language (EFL) teacher–researcher collaboration. *System*, *133*, 103757. https://doi.org/10.1016/j.system.2025.103757

Schindler, S. (2021). *Business research methods* (14th ed.). McGraw-Hill.

Schön, D. A. (1983). *The reflective practitioner: How professionals think in action*. Basic Books.

Scoupe, R., Delnoij, L., & Beausaert, S. (2024). Reflective practice among pre-service teachers: The role of portfolios. *Educational Research*, *66*(4), 429–447. https://doi.org/10.1080/00131881.2024.2412642

Senese, J. C. (2017). How do I know what I think I know? Teaching reflection to improve practice. In R. Brandenburg, S. McDonough, J. Burke, & S. White (Eds.), *Reflective theory and practice in teacher education* (pp. 103–118). Springer. https://doi.org/10.1007/978-981-10-3431-2_6

Seo, K., Yoo, M., Dodson, S., & Jin, S.-H. (2025). Augmented teachers: K–12 teachers' needs for artificial intelligence's complementary role in personalized learning. *Journal of Research on Technology in Education*, *57*(4), 876–893. https://doi.org/10.1080/15391523.2024.2330525

Sert, O. (2025). Partnering with AI in teacher education? Using an automatic question detection tool to reflect on classroom interaction. *Journal of Research on Technology in Education*. https://doi.org/10.1080/15391523.2025.2504355

Sharkey, N. E. (2012). The evitability of autonomous robot warfare. *International Review of the Red Cross*, *94*(886), 787–799. https://doi.org/10.1017/S1816383112000732

Sharkey, N., & Sharkey, A. (2010). The crying shame of robot nannies: An ethical appraisal. *Interaction Studies*, *11*(2), 161–190. https://doi.org/10.1075/is.11.2.01sha

Sharkey, A., & Sharkey, N. (2021). We need to talk about deception in social robotics! *Ethics and Information Technology*, *23*(3), 309–316. https://doi.org/10.1007/s10676-020-09573-9

Sheetal, A., Jiang, Z., & Di Milia, L. (2023). Using machine learning to analyze longitudinal data: A tutorial guide and best-practice recommendations for social science researchers. *Applied Psychology*, *72*(3), 1339–1364. https://doi.org/10.1111/apps.12435

Sheng, J., Amankwah-Amoah, J., Khan, Z., & Wang, X. (2021). COVID-19 pandemic in the new era of big data analytics: Methodological innovations and future research directions. *British Journal of Management*, *32*(4), 1164–1183. https://doi.org/10.1111/1467-8551.12441

Shor, R., Greene, E. A., Sumberg, L., & Weingrad, A. B. (2025). AI tools in academia: Evaluating NotebookLM as a tool for conducting literature reviews. *Psychiatry*. https://doi.org/10.1080/00332747.2025.2541531

Shrestha, Y. R., Ben-Menahem, S. M., & von Krogh, G. (2019). Organizational decision-making structures in the age of artificial intelligence. *California Management Review*, *61*(4), 66–83. https://doi.org/10.1177/0008125619862257

Siemon, D., Elshan, E., de Vreede, T., Ebel, P., & de Vreede, G.-J. (2025). Beyond anthropomorphism: Social presence in human–AI collaboration processes. *Journal of Management Studies*. https://doi.org/10.1111/joms.70000

Skubis, I. (2024a). *Ética, terminología, opiniones y el mercado de SexTech: un análisis multidisciplinario sobre los robots sexuales*. Politechniki Śląskiej.

Skubis, I. (2024b). Seksroboty – Zarządzanie etyką i zarządzanie innowacjami w branży sextech. *Management and Quality*, *6*(3), 211–232.

Skubis, I. (2024c). The EU guidelines on ethics of robots and sex robots. In C. Lütge, A. Kriebitz, R. Max & C. C. Corrigan (Eds.), *The Elgar companion to applied AI ethics* (pp. 397–408). Edward Elgar Publishing. https://doi.org/10.4337/9781803928241.00023

Skubis, I. (2025a). AI and leadership in the age of automation: A critical analysis of Generation Z's perspectives on humanoid robot leaders. *International Journal of Humanoid Robotics*, *22*(5), 2550006. https://doi.org/10.1142/S0219843625500069

Skubis, I. (2025b). Exploring the potential and perceptions of social robots in tourism and hospitality: Insights from industry executives and technology evaluation. *International Journal of Social Robotics*, *17*, 59–72. https://doi.org/10.1007/s12369-024-01197-z

Skubis, I. (2025c). Humanoid robots CEOs and leaders in project management: Decision-making, human oversight, team dynamics and ethics. *International Journal of Humanoid Robotics*, *22*(6), 2550008. https://doi.org/10.1142/S0219843625500082

Skubis, I., & Damas, K. (2025). Harnessing artificial intelligence in marketing: Comparative analysis of platforms and their features, capabilities, and applications. *Linguistic and Philosophical Investigations*, *24*(1), 43–60 https://philolinginvestigations.com/index.php/journal/article/view/465

Skubis, I., & Mosek, M. (2025). Human-like and humanoid virtual influencers (HVIs): Transforming digital marketing and consumer engagement. *Linguistic and Philosophical Investigations*, *24*(1), 170–190

Skubis, I., & Wodarski, K. (2023). Humanoid robots in managerial positions – Decision-making process and human oversight. *Scientific Papers of Silesian University of Technology – Organization and Management Series*, *189*, 573–596. http://doi.org/10.29119/1641-3466.2023.189.36

Skubis, I., Wodarski, K., & Boch, A. (2023). Language in the human-technology era. New terminology on the sex (robot) market – "digisexuality," "technosexuality" and "robosexuality" – a multilingual analysis and survey among students. *Scientific Papers of Silesian University of Technology – Organization and Management Series*, *189*, 553–572. http://doi.org/10.29119/1641-3466.2023.189.35

Skubis, I., Mesjasz-Lech, A., & Nowakowska-Grunt, J. (2024a). Humanoid robots in tourism and hospitality – Exploring managerial, ethical, and societal challenges. *Applied Sciences*, *14*(24), 11823. https://doi.org/10.3390/app142411823

Skubis, I., Wodarski, K., & Lütge, C. (2024b). Human–ChatGPT interaction: Prompt analysis on the basis of the sex robots' topic – Linguistic, social and ethical considerations of generative AI. *Linguistic and Philosophical Investigations*,

23(1), 2467–2485. https://philolinginvestigations.com/index.php/journal/article/view/413

Skubis, I., Wodarski, K., & Lütge, C. (2025). Ethical considerations, prompt management and linguistic challenges in ChatGPT's responses to controversial topics: A comparative analysis of GPT-3.5 and GPT-4.0 in the case study on sex robot influencers. *Review of Contemporary Philosophy*, *24*(1), 54–82. https://www.reviewofconphil.com/index.php/journal/article/view/1039

Smith, J. J., Yendol-Hoppey, D., & Milam, R. S. (2010). Reflectivity within the teacher research cycle: Promoting prospective teachers' progress toward an inquiry stance. In E. G. Pultorak (Ed.), *The purposes, practices, and professionalism of teacher reflectivity: Insights for twenty-first-century teachers and students* (pp. 15–31). Bloomsbury.

Soomro, A. F. (2018). Evaluating the significance of exploratory practice as an approach to teacher development. *Reflective Practice*, *19*(4), 461–473. https://doi.org/10.1080/14623943.2018.1519487

Sowa, K., & Przegalinska, A. (2025). From expert systems to generative artificial experts: A new concept for human–AI collaboration in knowledge work. *Journal of Artificial Intelligence Research*, *82*, 2101–2124. https://doi.org/10.1613/jair.1.17175

Standford Robotics Lab. (n.d.). *OceanOneK*. https://cs.stanford.edu/groups/manips/ocean-one-k.html

Steingard, D., & Rodenburg, K. (2025). Assessing the societal impact of academic research with artificial intelligence (AI): A scoping review of business school scholarship as a 'force for good'. *Learned Publishing*, *38*(3), e2010. https://doi.org/10.1002/leap.2010

Stenhouse, A., Fisher, N., Lepschi, B., Schmidt-Lebuhn, A., Rodriguez, J., Turco, F., Reeson, A., Paris, C., & Thrall, P. H. (2025). A vision of human–AI collaboration for enhanced biological collection curation and research. *BioScience*, *75*(6), 457–471. https://doi.org/10.1093/biosci/biaf021

Sterz, S., Baum, K., Biewer, S., Hermanns, H., Lauber-Rönsberg, A., Meinel, P., & Langer, M. (2024). On the quest for effectiveness in human oversight: Interdisciplinary perspectives. In *Proceedings of the ACM Conference on Fairness, Accountability, and Transparency (FAccT'24)* (pp. 1–13). ACM. https://doi.org/10.1145/3630106.3659051

Stokel-Walker, C., & Van Noorden, R. (2023). The promise and peril of generative AI. *Nature*, *614*, 214–216. https://doi.org/10.1038/d41586-023-00340-6

Sugihara, T., & Morisawa, M. (2020). A survey: dynamics of humanoid robots. *Advanced Robotics*, *34*(21–22), 1338–1352. https://doi.org/10.1080/01691864.2020.1778524

Sui, J., Zhang, Y., & Zhao, Y. (2025). Cultural tightness increases individuals' preference for control in human–AI collaboration. *International Journal of Human–Computer Interaction*. https://doi.org/10.1080/10447318.2025.2530079

Sun, X., & Song, Y. (2025). Unlocking the synergy: Increasing productivity through human–AI collaboration in the Industry 5.0 era. *Computers & Industrial Engineering*, *200*, 110657. https://doi.org/10.1016/j.cie.2024.110657

Sun, Z., Yu, Z. C., & Xu, F. Y. (2023). Analysis and improvement of classroom teaching based on artificial intelligence. In H. Niemi, J. Jia, Y. Lu, & M. Lavonen (Eds.), *AI in learning: Designing the future* (pp. 105–121). Springer. https://doi.org/10.1007/978-3-031-09687-7_7

Tambe, P., Cappelli, P., & Yakubovich, V. (2019). Artificial intelligence in human resources management: Challenges and a path forward. *California Management Review, 61*(4), 15–42. https://doi.org/10.1177/0008125619867910

Tazaki, Y., & Murooka, M. (2020). A survey of motion planning techniques for humanoid robots. *Advanced Robotics, 34*(21–22), 1370–1379. https://doi.org/10.1080/01691864.2020.1803128

The Economist. (2023, February 28). Investors are going nuts for ChatGPT-ish artificial intelligence. https://www.economist.com/business/2023/02/28/investors-are-going-nuts-for-chatgpt-ish-artificial-intelligence

Tong, Y., Liu, H., & Zhang, Z. (2024). Advancements in humanoid robots: A comprehensive review and future prospects. *IEEE/CAA Journal of Automatica Sinica, 11*(2), 301–328. https://doi.org/10.1109/JAS.2023.124140

Tong, D., Jin, B., Tao, Y., Ren, H., Islam, A. Y. M. A., & Bao, L. (2025). Exploring the role of human–AI collaboration in solving scientific problems. *Physical Review Physics Education Research, 21*, 010149. https://doi.org/10.1103/PhysRevPhysEducRes.21.010149

Tubis, A. A., & Rohman, J. (2023). Intelligent warehouse in Industry 4.0 – A systematic literature review. *Sensors, 23*(8), 4105. https://doi.org/10.3390/s23084105

Turakhia, D., Mroue, Z., Jiang, P., & Mueller, S. (2024). Generating reflection prompts in self-directed learning activities with generative AI. *An MIT Exploration of Generative AI.* https://doi.org/10.21428/e4baedd9.5970fe13

Vassilopoulou, J., Kyriakidou, O., Özbilgin, M. F., & Groutsis, D. (2024). Scientism as illusio in HR algorithms: Towards a framework for algorithmic hygiene for bias proofing. *Human Resource Management Journal, 34*(2), 311–325. https://doi.org/10.1111/1748-8583.12430

Vicente, L., & Cabitza, F. (2025). Machine mentoring by machine learning: Setting a research agenda on how human–AI collaboration can trigger knowledge and bias transmission. In M. Kurosu & A. Hashizume (Eds.), *Human-computer interaction* (pp. 72–94). Springer. https://doi.org/10.1007/978-3-031-93838-2_5

Wang, S., Chaovalitwongse, W., & Babuska, R. (2012). Machine learning algorithms in bipedal robot control. *IEEE Transactions on Systems, Man, and Cybernetics: Part C (Applications and Reviews), 42*(5), 728–743. https://doi.org/10.1109/TSMCC.2012.2186565

Wang, H., Luo, N., Zhou, T., & Yang, S. (2024). Physical robots in education: A systematic review based on the Technological Pedagogical Content Knowledge Framework. *Sustainability, 16*(12), 4987. https://doi.org/10.3390/su16124987

Wang, M., Long, T., Li, N., Shi, Y., & Chen, Z. (2025). The impact of different types of feedback on pre-service teachers' microteaching practice and perceptions. *Education and Information Technologies, 30*, 5427–5448. https://doi.org/10.1007/s10639-024-13024-z

Weed, J. (2023, March 16). Can ChatGPT plan your vacation? Here's what to know about A.I. and travel. *The New York Times.* https://www.nytimes.com/2023/03/16/travel/chatgpt-artificial-intelligence-travel-vacation.html

Wei, X., Wang, L., Koszalka, T. A., Lee, L.-K., & Liu, R. (2025). Enhancing pre-service teachers' reflective thinking skills through generative AI-assisted digital storytelling creation: A three-dimensional framework analysis. *Computers & Education, 235*, 105356. https://doi.org/10.1016/j.compedu.2025.105356

Williams, A. (2023, March 7). Which London universities ban ChatGPT and AI chatbots? *The Standard*. https://www.standard.co.uk/tech/london-universities-ban-chatgpt-ai-chatbots-plagiarisation-b1065331.html

Williams, E. (2025, July 31). "They built it to save lives" but Korea's Armstrong Dex robot throwing bottles sparks heated debate over rescue tech and the militarization of disaster response. *Energy Reporters*. https://www.energy-reporters.com/industry/they-built-it-to-save-lives-but-koreas-armstrong-dex-robot-throwing-bottles-sparks-heated-debate-over-rescue-tech-and-the-militarization-of-disaster-response/

WMA. (2013). World Medical Association Declaration of Helsinki: Ethical principles for medical research involving human subjects. *JAMA, 310*(20), 2191–2194. https://doi.org/10.1001/jama.2013.281053

Wołk, A., Skowrońska, H., & Skubis, I. (2021). Multilingual chatbot for e-commerce: Data generation and machine translation. In *PACIS 2021 proceedings* (Paper 232). https://aisel.aisnet.org/pacis2021/232

World Economic Forum. (2024). *The global risks report 2024: Insight report* (19th ed.). https://www.weforum.org/publications/global-risks-report-2024/

Xerri, D. (2017, July). Teacher research as creative disruption. *Modern English Teacher, 26*(3), 17–19.

Xerri, D. (2019). Researching teacher research. In G. Barkhuizen (Ed.), *Qualitative research topics in language teacher education* (pp. 174–179). Routledge. https://doi.org/10.4324/9780429461347-29

Xerri, D. (2021). Teacher research engagement. In H. Mohebbi & C. Coombe (Eds.), *Research questions in language education and applied linguistics: A reference guide* (pp. 767–771). Springer. https://doi.org/10.1007/978-3-030-79143-8_133

Xerri, D. (2022). *How can teachers best be encouraged to engage with research – published and their own practitioner inquiry?* British Council. https://www.teachingenglish.org.uk/sites/teacheng/files/2022-07/SUPPORTING_TEACHERS_TO_ENGAGE_WITH_RESEARCH.pdf

Xerri, D. (2024, Winter). Prompt engineering in language education: A practical guide. *ETAS Journal, 41*(2), 34–36. https://www.e-tas.ch/issues/winter-2024-2025/

Xerri, D. (2025a). AI in education: Challenges and opportunities. *Symposia Melitensia, 20*, 33–37. https://www.um.edu.mt/library/oar/bitstream/123456789/136264/1/AI_in_Education_Challenges_and_Opportunities_2025.pdf

Xerri, D. (2025b, January). Critical thinking as a cornerstone of a human-centred mindset towards AI use. *Learning Technologies SIG Newsletter*, 9–12.

Xerri, D. (2025c). Enhancing reflective practice in language teacher education: Technology as a critical reflective partner. *Technology in Language Teaching & Learning, 7*(2). https://doi.org/10.29140/tltl.v7n2.103214

Xerri, D. (2025d). Review of the book *Disseminating your action research: A practical guide to sharing the results of practitioner research*, by C. A. Mertler. *ELT Journal, 79*(2), 330–332. https://doi.org/10.1093/elt/ccaf004

Xerri, D., & Block, J. (2024). Learning to be a writing instructor in the age of generative AI: The role of research-practice partnerships. *Language Teacher Education Research, 1*, 64–68. https://doi.org/10.32038/lter.2024.01.04

Xerri, D., & Block, J. (2025). Unlocking teachers' generative AI-oriented professional learning through research–practice partnerships. *Teacher Development Academic Journal, 5*(1).

Xerri, D., & Pioquinto, C. (Eds.). (2018). *Becoming research literate: Supporting teacher research in English language teaching.* ETAS.

Xerri, D., Block, J., Boezio, J. L., & Davis, S. (2026). Liquid identities and generative AI: A research-practice partnership exploring English language teachers' integration of AI tools for teaching writing. In S. Wang Chong, H. Reinders, & Q. Liu (Eds.), *Research-practice partnership in language education.* Palgrave Macmillan.

Yan, Z., & Qianjun, T. (2025). Integrating AI-generated content tools in higher education: A comparative analysis of interdisciplinary learning outcomes. *Scientific Reports, 15*, 25802. https://doi.org/10.1038/s41598-025-10941-y

Yang, Y.-F., Tseng, C. C., & Lai, S.-C. (2024). Enhancing teachers' self-efficacy beliefs in AI-based technology integration into English speaking teaching through a professional development program. *Teaching and Teacher Education, 144.* https://doi.org/10.1016/j.tate.2024.104582

Yeh, H.-C. (2025). The synergy of generative AI and inquiry-based learning: Transforming the landscape of English teaching and learning. *Interactive Learning Environments, 33*(1), 88–102. https://doi.org/10.1080/10494820.2024.2335491

Yuan, R., Mak, P., & Yang, M. (2020). 'We teach, we record, we edit, and we reflect': Engaging pre-service language teachers in video-based reflective practice. *Language Teaching Research, 26*(3), 552–571. https://doi.org/10.1177/1362168820906281

Zeichner, K. M., & Liston, D. P. (2014). *Reflective teaching: An introduction* (2nd ed.). Routledge.

Zhang, C. (2024). *Fostering pre-service teacher reflection through AI-based feedback: From understanding AI acceptance to developing effective AI-driven feedback* [Doctoral dissertation, Friedrich-Alexander-Universität Erlangen-Nürnberg]. https://open.fau.de/handle/openfau/31410

Zhao, Z. J., Li, J., Hong, Y., & Yun, T. Y. (2025). Lesson study as an approach to facilitate the integration of Gen-AI into EFL curriculum design in higher education. *International Journal for Lesson & Learning Studies.* https://doi.org/10.1108/IJLLS-01-2025-0029

Zilber, A. (2025, July 28). Robot tosses water bottle into barrel from across the room to pass key disaster relief test. *New York Post.* https://nypost.com/2025/07/28/business/robot-tosses-water-bottle-into-barrel-to-pass-key-disaster-relief-test/

Złotowski, J., Yogeeswaran, K., & Bartneck, C. (2017). Can we control it? Autonomous robots threaten human identity, uniqueness, safety, and resources. *International Journal of Human-Computer Studies, 100*, 48–54. https://doi.org/10.1016/j.ijhcs.2016.12.008

Zwozdiak-Myers, P. N. (2024). *The teacher's reflective practice handbook: Becoming an extended professional through capturing evidence-informed practice* (2nd ed.). Routledge.

Index

A

B

H

I

L

M

N

O

P

R

S

T

For Product Safety Concerns and Information please contact our EU representative GPSR@taylorandfrancis.com Taylor & Francis Verlag GmbH, Kaufingerstraße 24, 80331 München, Germany